THE PRIESTHOOD

BY

THE MOST REV. WILHELM STOCKUMS, D.D.

Auxiliary Bishop of Cologne

TRANSLATED BY

THE REV. JOSEPH W. GRUNDNER

TAN BOOKS AND PUBLISHERS, INC.
Rockford, Illinois 61105

NIHIL OBSTAT

Sti. Ludovici, die 4. Jan., 1938,

F. J. Holweck,
Censor Librorum

IMPRIMATUR

Sti. Ludovici, die 5. Jan., 1938,

✠ Joannes J. Glennon,
Archiepiscopus

TAN BOOKS AND PUBLISHERS, INC.
P.O. Box 424
Rockford, Illinois 61105

1974

Foreword

The late Bishop Francis C. Kelley in his inspiring book *Dominus Vobiscum* wrote the following familiar words: "There is something all but overwhelming in the thought of the dignity and the power and the office we priests of God bear. There is enough of dread and awe in it to crush us. And yet, it is the knowledge and the realization of it that makes us better and happier, more faithful and more fruitful priests. Show me a lax, a discontented and unfaithful priest, and I will show you one who has forgotten the greatness of his calling, the sublimity of his dignity and the awesomeness of his God-given powers for true and lasting good for countless souls redeemed by the Precious Blood of the Saviour of the world."

Now, despite the fact that from the earliest centuries the Catholic Church has spoken to us—and repeatedly, in the name of the Great High Priest, Jesus Christ—of the nature and purpose and of the exalted dignity and tremendous powers of the priesthood and those who share in it, and done so, through her early Fathers and Doctors and (how frequently and eloquently) through her great theologians and spiritual writers, through the holy Vicars of Jesus Christ, and through her many Councils; despite her numerous solemn and authoritative pronouncements, these nearly twenty centuries, on the meaning, the excellence and the special work of the priesthood and of the priest, we repeat, there have been these past eight years all too many priests of God who have experienced a certain loss of identity (a "crisis of identity," they call it), so that these chosen and consecrated privileged ones of the Lord God have questioned the reality, the augustness, and the purpose of their divine vocation as "shepherds, prophets, and priests of the People of God." Moreover, they have blinded themselves to the real nature of their sanctifying and saving priestly talents, and to the value, the relevance, and the necessity of the spiritual treasures they have been called, sanctified, consecrated, and empowered to dispense to men—treasures which bring glory to God in the highest, and peace and salvation to men on earth, treasures which have been needed and yearned for by men in every age, and perhaps, never needed more desperately and longed for more ardently than by men in the turbulent, confused, and materialistic world of this last third of the twentieth century.

How can men so highly favored and so richly equipped by Almighty God forget what they are, what God has done for them, and what He expects them to be and to do? How can any of them ever abandon their glorious priesthood—that priesthood which is "indispensable to the bringing of Jesus Christ and His salvation to a world redeemed by Him?"

How? Why? There may be, and doubtless are, many reasons. Certainly, one is the following. During the past decade, priests have been deluged with books and with articles in various periodicals which downgrade and even falsify the *essential nature, purpose, and duties* of this most divine of all vocations—a calling, a vocation, a ministry so exalted and awesome that a greater one cannot be conceived.

Twenty-five years ago Cardinal Suhard wrote a monumental pastoral letter on the holy priesthood (*Priests among Men*). There his Eminence proposed and convincingly defended the thesis that modern man's search for God, His truth, and His salvation, would be in vain unless this quest were accompanied by a rediscovery of the priesthood. And he concluded that there would be no return to God without a return to the priest, that is without a recognition of "the minister of Christ and the dispenser of the Mysteries of God," and an acceptance of the treasures of truth and life, of holiness and peace, which the Catholic priest is divinely commissioned and empowered to bring to men through his God-given, peerless talents "to offer Sacrifice, to bless, to preach, to shepherd and to administer the Sacraments, or the channels of grace, to souls."

In our own day and age, we priests must again and again, remind ourselves about and vividly realize *the essential meaning and purpose* of the priesthood of Jesus Christ, in which we have been given a share. To help us remember and appreciate what God has done for us, and what He demands that we be and do, I know of no finer book than *The Priesthood,* written by the late Auxiliary Bishop of Cologne, his Excellency the Most Reverend Wilhelm Stockums. Its nine chapters on the nature and essence of the priesthood are the most inspiring, eloquent, and convincing pages I have ever read on this most exalted of all vocations. The book is a masterpiece, and if I were a bishop I would see to it that a copy of it were in the hands of each of my priests. And if I were a seminary rector I would do all I could to place a copy in the hands of every member of my faculty and of each of my students.

The clergy and also the laity of the Church in the United States owe a deep debt of gratitude to the TAN Books and Publishers, Inc. of Rockford, Illinois for reprinting Bishop Stockums' classic and for making it available at so reasonable a price. It is our confident hope and prayer that through the grace of our Great High Priest, Jesus Christ, and through the intercession of Mary, the Queen of the clergy, this book will help all of us priests to understand and appreciate the holy priesthood with an ever-increasing faith, to embrace it with an ever-increasing humility, to love it with an ever-increasing fervor, and to live it with an ever-increasing fidelity, and that it will inspire more and more of our young men to leave all things, to enter the seminary, and to prepare themselves earnestly to become "the presence and the power of Jesus Christ" among men.

John M. Dougherty, S.S.,
St. Charles' Villa,
Baltimore, Maryland

June 19, 1974
Feast of St. Juliana Falconieri

Contents

CHAPTER   PAGE

I. THE DIVINE ORIGIN OF THE PRIESTHOOD 1

    The Priesthood as the Direct Institution of Christ   1

    The General and the Particular Priesthood . . 13

II. THE ESSENCE AND PURPOSE OF THE PRIESTHOOD . . 20

    The Priesthood of Christ. 20

    The Essential Tasks of the Priest 25

    The Supernatural Character of the Priest . . . 39

III. THE SUBLIME DIGNITY OF THE PRIESTHOOD . . . 43

    Source and Essence 43

    Participation in the Priesthood of Christ . . . 45

    Power over the Real Body of Christ. 49

    Power over the Mystical Body of Christ . . . 53

    Passages from the Church Fathers and Later Theologians 57

IV. THE PRIESTHOOD IN THE LIGHT OF THE NEW TESTAMENT 64

    "Salt of the Earth and Light of the World" . . 65

    "Man of God" 70

    "Pattern of the Flock" 75

    "Good Soldier of Jesus Christ" 78

    "Minister of Christ and Dispenser of the Mysteries of God" 81

    "Ambassador of Christ" 85

    "Mediator of God and Men". 88

iii

CHAPTER   PAGE

V. THE PRIESTHOOD AND THE CHURCH 92

What Does the Priesthood Accomplish for the
Church? 93

What Does the Church Do for the Priesthood? . 100

What Should Be the Personal Attitude of the
Priest toward the Church? 109

VI. THE PRIESTHOOD AND THE PEOPLE 115

The Social Character of the Priesthood. . . . 115

The Priest as the Shepherd of Souls. 120

VII. THE PRIESTHOOD AND THE WORLD 132

Tension and Opposition 132

Meaning and Purpose of the Priest's Renunciation
of the World. 138

Necessity of Renunciation of Self and of the
World 141

Deeper Motivation for Renunciation of the World 147

Conclusions for the Seminarian 155

VIII. THE PRIESTHOOD AND THE PRIEST 160

Close Connection 160

The Priesthood as a Source of Blessing to the
Priest 164

Special Dangers to Salvation in the Priesthood . 180

IX. THE PERSONAL SANCTIFICATION OF THE PRIEST . . 200

The Objective Holiness of the Priesthood . . . 200

Sacramental Consecration of the Priest's Person . 205

The Admonitions of St. Paul 209

Testimony of the Fathers and of the Church . . 217

Nature and Extent of Priestly Sanctification . . 222

INDEX 231

Chapter I

The Divine Origin of the Priesthood

I. THE PRIESTHOOD AS THE DIRECT INSTITUTION OF CHRIST

1. The Catholic priesthood comprises a homogeneous, exclusive, world-wide group of consecrated persons drawn from the most diverse races and nations, and constitutes a vocational state of life that is unique. From an external and social point of view, the priesthood may be classed among the higher professions; yet, in origin and essence, in mission and purpose, it differs utterly from all mundane vocations. The various earthly pursuits, from the humblest to the loftiest, from the purely mechanical to the scientific and artistic which embody and express the highest achievements of human culture, all owe their origin and development, their rise and decline, to the economic, social, and cultural conditions of the times. Changes in these conditions have in the course of the ages produced new mechanical and new intellectual vocations, but have also brought about the decline of previously existing ones, according as fresh needs emerged or former needs disappeared.

This continuous rise and decline, which is common to all mundane vocations, demonstrates more clearly than anything else how deeply they are rooted in the activity of the world. Some of these callings are as old as mankind and may almost be called a natural necessity. But even these last have been subject at least to a powerful development, and continue to be exposed to such variations down to our own day.

In contrast to these worldly professions, the Catholic priesthood appears as a vocational state that is not embedded in the fluctuating stream of human life or influenced by it. Untouched by the course of time and by changing conditions, it looms up in the history of mankind as an unchanging and unchangeable power. Of course, this state of life also has its external history, a development with its high and low points, but since its inception it has remained essentially the same through the ages. The Catholic priesthood, in its passage through nineteen centuries of the world's history, has in every age borne the marks of the times upon its outward habiliments; but in spite of all revolutionary changes among the nations it has never changed in its inner core or essence. In this respect the priesthood shares in the prerogative of the Catholic faith and of the Catholic Church, which likewise have never changed in any essential manner since the days of Christ.

The deep-lying explanation of this fact is that the priesthood, like the Church, did not evolve from the temporal and earthly needs of mankind. It was not fashioned by the hand of man, but by the hand of God. Christ Himself, the eternal Son of God, is the one who called the priesthood into existence. He planted it in the world as a tender shoot that was to unfold in the course of time to become a world-embracing tree. He alone is the founder of the New Testament priesthood. He has given it meaning and purpose, and placed it in the center of the supernatural organization established by Him for the salvation of mankind.

2. Naturally, what has been said does not mean that the world knew nothing of a priesthood until the time of Christ. A priesthood, in the broad sense of a group of official religious ministers, existed among the peoples of the world from the beginning and was an accompaniment of man's natural aptitude for religion. Hence, in so far as we have obtained a knowledge of the ancient nature religions, we learn that priests and priestesses were present in all of them. Among all peoples and in all ages we find altars on which sacrifices were offered to divinities by the hands of priests. To this extent the priesthood, taken in its most general meaning, is as old as humanity itself. In primitive cultures the priests constituted in many ways a highly influential caste; even in advanced and highly developed civilizations, as with the ancient Greeks and Romans, we come upon a priesthood that was of decisive significance for the religious life of those peoples. This type of priesthood was also a natural product, growing out of natural religious ideas and needs, and closely connected with the structure of ancient peoples. When the nations of antiquity passed away, this priesthood disappeared with them.

The ancient pagan priesthood gave visible expression to the relationship of man to God, so deeply rooted in human nature. By its manifold functions, especially by the offering of sacrifice, it definitely fostered the idea of man's connection with God, and lent symbol and form to the general, if vague, desire which human nature felt for the Deity. By means of altar, priest, and sacrifice, ancient mankind wished to preserve a vivid consciousness of its divine origin and its responsibility to God. In this limited sense, the ancient pagan priesthood may be spoken of as a shadowy type of the Christian priesthood, at least with regard to the idea of propitiation.

The last statement of the preceding paragraph is true in much greater degree of the priesthood of Israel, which, according to the express intention of God, was to foreshadow and prepare the way for the true priesthood of the New Testament. The Israelitic priesthood, founded and organized by Moses according to the instructions given by God, constituted not only a special state but also an exclusive confraternity based on blood-relationship in one particular tribe, inasmuch as it was limited to the progeny of Aaron and propagated by carnal procreation. But even this priesthood, willed by Jahve Himself and highly developed, this priesthood with its temple, its many sacrifices, and its elaborate ritual, had only a temporary and typical significance. It came to an end automatically, when the true and perfect High Priest of all mankind appeared in the person of Jesus Christ. In that moment the Jewish priesthood had completed its mission.

Now that the ancient pagan and the Israelitic priesthoods have disappeared from among mankind, leaving behind them merely a historical memory of vanished greatness, only one priesthood continues to exist among civilized peoples— the priesthood established in the Catholic Church by Christ. In the civilized nations of the present, including the non-Christian peoples, we indeed find no lack of religious ministers, preachers, and spiritual leaders, but they are not really priests. The only priests who can lay claim to this title in the strict sense of the word are found today in Catholic Christianity. Lippert rightly remarks: "At any rate they have not developed as a natural product of the social evolution of mankind; if that were the case, they would have passed away as did the priesthoods of the nature religions. Christian priests are the creation of a single Man, of an omnipotent Man who in His infinite power towered above all the laws of nature; they are an institution created and established by Jesus Christ." [1]

3. Christ, the Son of God, is the founder of the new, the Christian priesthood. He Himself is the new High Priest foretold by the prophets, the eternal Priest, not according to the order of Aaron but according to the order of Melchisedech. He received His priestly consecration by the coming of the Holy Spirit at the moment of His incarnation—at the very beginning, therefore, of His life as God-man—and His highest priestly act, in fact His only priestly function, was performed at the very end of His life when, dying on the cross, He offered to His heavenly Father the sacrifice of the atonement.

Christ made His appearance on this earth as a being wholly novel, as a being from another world, as the consubstantial Son of God Himself. Of this earth He assumed only His bodily form, His external appearance. Even though, to outward seeming, He had come forth from the race of men, still the essence of His being and His personality, precisely that which constituted His person, was eternal and divine. And so, He stands in the world of men as a being who is unique, as the Son of God and the Son of man in one person.

In an analogous manner, the same is true of the institu-

[1] *Vom guten Menschen* (1931), p. 228.

tions of Christ: the Church and specifically the priesthood. In creating a new priesthood He indeed made use of existing elements, especially those found in the Israelitic priesthood, but not with the purpose of modifying the latter and then perpetuating it in His kingdom. As a matter of fact, He took over only the outward appearance and form, and the external functions of that priesthood into His new creation, giving this appearance and form, however, an essentially different content and meaning. By virtue of His divine plenitude of power He abolished, systematically and for all time, the entire Old Testament order of sacrifice; in place of those typical offerings which had accomplished their purpose, He set up a new and eternal sacrifice, the offering up of which He committed to the hands of new priests, called by Him.[2]

Therefore the Catholic priesthood is far from being a later development of the priesthood of Aaron. Like Christ Himself, it entered the stream of evolution as something altogether new and positive, as something that made its appearance in the world of men from the world of God, and was never henceforth to disappear from this earth. To speak again with Lippert: "Hence, Catholic priests are, as it were, grafted upon the ancient tree of mankind from without, they have not grown out of it; they have been generated by a free act, not by an unconscious development; they constitute, therefore, a break in the continuous stream of evolution; they are something new and unique suddenly taking its place in the chain of phenomena. But even though they have come from without, they are now and henceforth a link in the chain, a tributary to the great stream of mankind's life, a branch on this tree, and by an exchange of strength, by a

[2] Cf. *Cat. Rom.*, II, cap. 7, q. 8.

mutual give and take, they stand in organic connection with the whole in which they live." [3]

Such, in truth, is the characteristic and unique feature in the phenomenon of the Catholic priesthood. Even though it has penetrated mankind as something strange and novel, it has nevertheless entered into the closest association with mankind and constitutes an indispensable cultural factor, as well as a salutary source of strength and power for the whole. This condition is simply an indication of the intimate connection that exists between the true progress and the last end of mankind on the one hand, and the purposes and tasks of Christianity in general and of the priesthood in particular on the other.

4. If we wish to grasp more clearly the real essence of the priesthood, we must go back to Christ, its source, and ask about the meaning of His own appearance in the world and of His mission. The life and labor of Jesus had no natural or earthly significance. They tower far above the human order into the lofty, supernatural world of God. Redemption from sin and guilt, the gaining of grace and salvation for mankind, the reconciliation of fallen humanity with its God and Creator, eternal bliss for the privileged souls of men—all these constitute the profound spiritual purpose of the life, the ministry, and the death of Christ.

But this divine work of redemption, realized by a single act of atonement, could not be and was not permitted to be limited by time or place in its operation. Its tendency was to the universal and the timeless; it was to embrace all men of all lands and of all times, and win them to eternal salvation. According to the eternal, world-embracing plan of divine

[3] *Loc. cit.*

Providence, the teaching and the grace of God were to reach all generations on earth. To this end the work of redemption had to find a mystical and living continuation and operation that would perdure until the end of time.

Viewed from this angle, the deeper and essential idea of the Church, and in particular of the priesthood, becomes manifest. Why did Christ institute the Church and the priesthood? Why were they so necessary? Both institutions were necessary because they were to take over the mediation of grace and salvation. In this sense the Church, as St. Paul was the first to grasp clearly, is the mystical Christ living on and continuing His work. And the priesthood within the Church? It was to take over the direct mediation of salvation in the name and person of Christ; it was to be the living instrument in the hands of the Son of God, the instrument by which He would guide the streams of grace to the souls of men. Since the Church as an organic whole is the mystical body of Christ and since Christ Himself is the head of that body, then we may appropriately designate the priesthood as the pulsating heart of that body. From the priesthood the stream of supernatural life flows through the Church; the priesthood is the fountain and source from which all graces and blessings come to the individual members of Christ's mystical body. Our Lord did not confer the priestly dignity upon all who accepted His Gospel and were admitted into the communion of His faithful. On the contrary, He elevated only a few from the general status of children of God to this new dignity; to those chosen few He transmitted His own supernatural power for the salvation of men. In addition to the teaching and pastoral office, Christ instituted also the priestly office whose function was to renew, in all times and places and in an unbloody manner, His great atonement sacrifice and to make its fruits available to all men.

5. That Christ had the definite intention of instituting a special consecrated priesthood, distinct from the laity in general, is proved, first of all, by the account of the striking manner in which He chose the Apostles. As the Evangelists (especially St. Luke 6: 12 f. and St. Mark 3: 13) relate in detail, our Lord advanced to this task after careful reflection and with great deliberation. The calling took place in the early morning, after He had passed the preceding night in prayer on the mountain top. "And when day was come, he called unto him his disciples; and he chose twelve of them (whom also he named apostles)," is the way St. Luke's account reads. St. Mark lays special emphasis upon the circumstance that He chose those "whom he would himself." Accordingly, not all those who believed in Him and followed Him, not even all the disciples, nor those of the latter who had perhaps pushed themselves forward, were admitted into the sacred circle of specially chosen ones, but only those upon whom His own voluntary choice had fallen. The names of the Twelve are then carefully listed, a testimony to the fact that the event had aroused the particular attention of the bystanders, and especially of the chosen ones themselves.

And, in truth, the selection of the Apostles merits our closest attention inasmuch as it goes beyond the founding of the New Testament priesthood and marks the institution of the Church's hierarchy of which the priesthood is only a part. Precisely because Christ Himself was fully aware of the overshadowing importance of His action, He prepared Himself for it by a night of recollection and prayer. Peering with divine eyes into the distant future, He saw that the men

He would choose and their successors in the episcopal and priestly office would be the heart and backbone of His Church.

In the time that followed the selection of the Apostles the Master lavished all His care and love upon the twelve chosen ones. With particular zeal He labored to bring them to an understanding of His teaching and the mysteries of the Gospel. They tarried continuously in His presence, they had the daily inspiration of His sublime example, they became His intimates, His dearest friends, joined to Him by the bond of a deep and ardent love. He was the Master and Teacher, they the docile and obedient pupils. This apostolic school was the first priestly seminary, a seminary in which the divine High Priest Himself was rector, teacher, and model.

To these preferred disciples, and to them alone, the Master on successive occasions directed those memorable sentences in which He transmitted His divine powers. The words He spoke to the Twelve have the flavor of another world and stand out as if chiseled in imperishable stone by the hand of God:

"As the Father hath sent me, I also send you." [4]

"He that heareth you, heareth me; and he that despiseth you, despiseth me; and he that despiseth me, despiseth him that sent me." [5]

"All power is given to me in heaven and in earth. Going therefore, teach ye all nations; baptizing them in the name of the Father, and of the Son, and of the Holy Ghost, teaching them to observe all things whatsoever I have commanded

[4] John 20: 21.
[5] Luke 10: 16.

you: and behold I am with you all days even to the consummation of the world." [6]

"Whose sins you shall forgive, they are forgiven them; and whose sins you shall retain, they are retained." [7]

"Amen I say to you, whatsoever you shall bind upon earth, shall be bound also in heaven; and whatsoever you shall loose upon earth, shall be loosed also in heaven." [8]

"Do this for a commemoration of me." [9]

When we allow these phrases to pass in review before our minds, the truth is brought home to us that Christ desired to stress with all possible emphasis the parity between the mission that He had received from His heavenly Father and the mission that was to go out from Him to His Apostles. Especially with the last words quoted above, words spoken toward the end of the last supper, our Lord clothed the Apostles with the fulness of priestly consecratory and sacrificial power. As indicated by the word "this," they were empowered to do precisely what He had just done before their eyes, that is, to celebrate a holy, sacrificial meal, in which they too, and indeed in His name, would with miraculous effect say over the bread and wine: "This is my body; this is my blood."

6. The Church has always taught that Christ instituted a new priesthood. Against the objections and attacks of the so-called reformers of the sixteenth century, she formulated this teaching anew, and the Council of Trent proclaimed it again in solemn, dogmatic form: "Sacrifice and priesthood are so joined together by the ordinance of God, that both are

[6] Matt. 28: 18–20.
[7] John 20: 23.
[8] Matt. 18: 18.
[9] Luke 22: 19.

present in every dispensation. Therefore, since through the institution of the Lord the Catholic Church received in the New Testament the holy and visible sacrifice of the Eucharist, we must also concede that there exists in her a new, visible, and external priesthood, into which the old has been converted. Sacred Scripture shows and the tradition of the Catholic Church has always taught that this priesthood was instituted by the same Lord, our Savior, and that to the Apostles and their successors in the priesthood was granted the power to consecrate, to offer, and to dispense the body and blood of the Lord, and also to forgive and to retain sins." [10]

In this pronouncement of the Council of Trent we find mention, among other things, of the transition of the Old Testament priesthood into that of the New, and the latter is then described as a visible and external priesthood. As we have indicated above, a priesthood, established by God, existed in the Old Testament and constituted the vital center of the religious community life of Israel. But, just as the entire Old Testament was only a preparation for the New Covenant and was destined to be replaced by the latter, so also the Old Testament priesthood had significance only as the first and transitional step to the final and absolute priesthood of the New Law; to the latter was committed the celebration of the Eucharist as a perpetual sacrifice. Israel's priesthood ceased to exist as a divinely established institution at the moment when the Son of God offered Himself as the bloody sacrifice of reparation. When the high priest Caiphas, at the trial of Jesus before the Sanhedrin, solemnly tore his garment, he performed an action that, without his own in-

[10] *Conc. Trid.*, Sess. XXIII, cap. 1, *de Ord.*

tent or knowledge, symbolized the destruction of the Old Testament priesthood. The last high priest of the Old Law was juridically retired from office in precisely that moment when the new High Priest, in the person of Christ, stood before him and prepared to consummate the great act of His new priesthood in the sacrifice of the cross—the former lending Him unwitting but most effective assistance by imposing the death sentence. It was indeed a memorable hour when these two high priests confronted each other, the one to bury his dignity and power, the other to inaugurate the new and eternal priesthood.

2. THE GENERAL AND THE PARTICULAR PRIESTHOOD

1. The New Testament priesthood, as the Council of Trent goes on to declare, is external and visible, instituted as such by Christ Himself. Everyone knows that early and modern Protestantism denies a visible church and also a visible priesthood. It acknowledges only an invisible ecclesiastical community of saints, and, since a visible priesthood has no place in such a conception, the latter dissolves into a so-called general and mystical priesthood to which all believers belong. The attempt is made to base this conception chiefly on St. Peter's words addressed to the faithful: "But you are a chosen generation, a kingly priesthood, a holy nation, a purchased people." [11] However, to assume that the Prince of the Apostles intended with these words to exclude the priesthood of orders is an error. Sound exegesis shows that the expression " a kingly priesthood," which goes back to Exodus 19: 6, is to be understood only in a general, meta-

[11] See I Pet. 2: 9.

phorical sense, inasmuch as all Christians, being children of God and co-heirs of Christ, are called to a kingly, priestly dignity. "Just as the general priestly dignity of all Israelites did not exclude the existence of a special priestly class, so also in the New Testament." [12]

The Catholic viewpoint has at all times steadfastly maintained the existence of a visible church, a visible sacrifice, and a visible and external priesthood, not of course in an exclusive sense, as if these institutions had only a visible side without an inner, invisible content. On the contrary, the invisible, essential side always remains the important thing.

2. With Holy Scripture, the Catholic Church also recognizes a twofold priesthood: an internal, invisible, general priesthood and an external, visible, specific priesthood; that is, a general priesthood of the laity and a special priesthood of orders. To the first belong all the faithful who have received the sacrament of baptism; they may be called priests in a metaphorical sense. To this priesthood belong in particular all the just who bear within themselves the Spirit of God and are living members of the mystical body of Christ, the divine High Priest. Their priestly functions are their acts of love of God and neighbor, performed with the aid of grace and offered to God as a spiritual sacrifice. The altar, that is, the place where the sacrifice of this interior, spiritual priesthood is offered is, as it were, the individual's heart, where his good intentions and good works are offered up to God.

This is the sense in which we must understand the quoted passage from the Epistle of St. Peter. The same is true of

[12] Felton, *Die zwei Briefe des hl. Petrus und der Judas brief* (1929), p. 79.

another sentence in the same letter, in which the Prince of the Apostles admonishes the Christians: "Be you also as living stones built up, a spiritual house, a holy priesthood, to offer up spiritual sacrifices, acceptable to God by Jesus Christ." [13]

In like manner and in the same metaphorical and spiritual sense the Apostle St. Paul addresses the following impressive exhortation to the Christians in Rome: "I beseech you therefore, brethren, by the mercy of God that you present your bodies a living sacrifice, holy, pleasing unto God, your reasonable service." [14]

The Apocalypse also recognizes the spiritual priesthood of all Christians in the words: "And from Jesus Christ, who . . . hath loved us and washed us from our sins in his own blood, and hath made us a kingdom, and priests to God and his Father." [15]

In the liturgy of the mass we also perceive the idea of a general priesthood to which every baptized person is called; and the thought of a joint offering of the sacrifice by priest and people is as much a part and as primitive a part of the mass liturgy as anything else. In many ways and very clearly the liturgical texts, all of them very ancient, designate the holy sacrifice of the mass as a sacrifice of the whole congregation whose representative is the consecrated priest at the altar. The use of the plural, a form which the celebrant employs throughout the canon of the mass, points to the active participation of the faithful in his priestly action.

After the offering of the bread and wine has been made,

[13] See I Pet. 2: 5.
[14] Rom. 12: 1.
[15] Apoc. 1: 5 f.

the priest says to the people: "Brethren, pray that my sacrifice and yours may be acceptable to God the Father almighty." Before the consecration and in direct connection with the *memento* for the living, the priest prays to God for all who are standing about the altar and who with him are offering the sacrifice of praise to God: "for whom we offer or who offer up to thee this sacrifice of praise for themselves and theirs." In like manner a little later, when the priest stretches out his hands over the *oblata,* he describes them as the common gift of himself and the people: "this offering of our bounden duty, as also of thy whole household." Again, after the consecration, the communal character of this offering made by the holy household of God and the consecrated priest who stands in its midst is clearly expressed in the words of the first prayer: "we thy servants, as also thy holy people," the last phrase obviously a reference to the *gens sancta* of I Pet. 2: 9. However, the significant thing about all these passages is that, while on the one hand they indeed emphasize the close connection between priest and congregation, they no less clearly make the officiating priest appear as the celebrant who, by virtue of a higher consecration, stands beside the people and at the same time above the people.

The invisible priesthood, therefore, is by no means a new discovery of Protestantism, but is as old as the New Testament; in fact, it even goes back to the Old Testament, where we find in the psalms mention of a spiritual sacrifice: "A sacrifice to God is an afflicted spirit: a contrite and humble heart, O God, thou wilt not despise." [16]

When we compare the quoted texts of the Old and New

16 Ps. 50: 19.

Testaments with one another, we cannot doubt that the meaning is always the same—almost the identical phrases recur—and the meaning is simply a stressing of the internal, spiritual priesthood, by which, however, the external and visible priesthood existing beside it was by no means excluded in either Testament. The fatal error of the so-called reformers consisted in this, that they put a wrong construction on these texts and interpreted them in an exclusive sense in order to further their innovations by eliminating the external, hierarchical priesthood. More far-sighted Protestants, right down to our own day, have been painfully aware of the irreparable loss that Protestantism has sustained by rejecting the priesthood of orders and the hierarchy.

Although the Catholic Church has always esteemed the general, spiritual priesthood of the laity, regarding it as the characteristic expression of the lofty, supernatural endowment and vocation of the individual Christian, she has in addition to it and at all times clung fast to the special external priesthood, a priesthood that in the pages of the New Testament and especially in the Pauline Epistles stands out in bold contrast to the general priesthood. The external priesthood is the one established by Christ Himself; it is conferred not upon all the faithful, but only upon certain men, and indeed by the lawful imposition of hands, that is, by the sacrament of holy orders.[17]

3. When the Church in her teaching lays emphasis upon the visible and external side of the priesthood, thereby separating the priesthood of orders as a distinct state from the general, invisible priesthood of the laity, she pursues the same course by which in other matters she distinguishes be-

[17] Cf. *Cat Rom.*, II, cap. 7, q.22.

tween visible and invisible, external and internal things. Both the creations of God in nature and the institutions of Christ in the order of supernature present this dual side of being. We may mention, for example, that man, the crown of earthly creation, possesses an invisible soul as well as a visible body. In the supernatural order the Church exists as a visible, external phenomenon, "a city seated on a mountain." [18] Visible are her life and work, her development and history, while her inner spiritual power, the operation of the Holy Spirit in and through her, is withdrawn from the eyes of men. The sacraments also are visible, being external and sensible signs to which the interior effect of grace is attached. Lastly, the Son of God in His human manifestation was visible to men, whereas His divine nature remained veiled and hidden. The priesthood likewise manifests these two aspects. Protestantism, in its conception of church and priesthood, made the fundamental mistake of placing a one-sided emphasis upon the internal factor and of showing no understanding at all for the external factor.

Recalling the main thought of the preceding considerations, we repeat that, according to the true or Catholic conception, the visible priesthood of orders was directly instituted by Christ, destined to serve the supernatural ends of the Christian religion. Hence the priesthood is in the truest sense "by the grace of God," and in its divine origin lie the sublimity and the inexhaustible power of this state. Something of the dignity and the greatness of its Institutor, something of His divinity, went over into His institution. Just as, in His divine majesty and grandeur, He towers infinitely above all that is earthly and human, just as His coming and

[18] Matt. 5: 14.

mission were directed solely to the sphere of the supernatural, so the priesthood, like its divine Founder, is indeed in the world and for the world, but not of the world. It did not originate in the world; in spite of the yearning that men of all times have felt for altar, priest, and sacrifice, it did not spring from the lap of mankind. On the contrary, the priesthood as it exists and operates in the Catholic Church was planted in the world as a heavenly seed by the hand of God's Son. Hence its origin is in an eminent sense divine and supernatural.

CHAPTER II

The Essence and Purpose of the Priesthood

I. THE PRIESTHOOD OF CHRIST

1. *Sacerdos alter Christus.* This ancient and venerable phrase expresses both a fact and a counsel. The fact consists in this, that every incumbent of the priestly office is by virtue of sacramental consecration another Christ in his supernatural life and vocation; and the counsel indicates that he should be another Christ in the moral order also by his personal life of virtue. The full meaning of the phrase is therefore threefold: mystical in regard to the priest's resemblance to Christ in the supernatural order, vocational in regard to his office, and moral in regard to his personal life.

It is indeed correct to say that this title of honor may not be claimed exclusively by the priest. The designation really fits every true follower of Christ, everyone who is a Christian not merely in name but is united to Christ by grace, everyone whose soul is permeated with the spirit and life of the Master. Every Christian, by his status as a child of God, has acquired a certain essential likeness to Christ, the only begotten Son of God, and has thereby assumed the moral obligation of conforming himself as closely as possible to the "first-born amongst many brethren." [1]

Since, therefore, we have no way of expressing more aptly or more profoundly the essence and scope of a true Christian character than by calling the Christian "another Christ," then surely we have no other phrase, no other honorary title, no other counsel, that can more clearly or more comprehensively describe the significance and mission of the Catholic priest. In a far higher and fuller sense than is true of the average Christian, the priest must be an *alter Christus*. Unlike the layman, he is placed in the closest relationship with Christ by his whole vocational activity. Priest and priesthood stand and fall with Christ. They are so intimately connected with Him in nature and purpose that, separated from Christ, they could not exist; in fact, they could not even be imagined, much less comprehended.

If we wish to acquire a clear understanding of the meaning and purpose of the Catholic priesthood, to appreciate its mission, and to discover its right to existence in the world of men, we must proceed from this fundamental relationship of the priest to Christ. This relationship provides the best approach to the question: What is the Catholic priest and what does he signify? From this viewpoint, also, we can best establish and appreciate the duty of personal sanctification incumbent upon every priest.

In the first place, the phrase "another Christ" designates the higher mystical order of existence and vocation in which the consecrated priest stands in relation to Christ and which raises the priesthood of orders far above the general priesthood of the laity. Christ's life and nature, His messianic vo-

[1] Rom. 8: 29.

cation, His divine mission, His sacrifice, and His high priesthood are the luminous factors that cast a clarifying light
upon the phenomenon of the New Testament priesthood,
its nature, structure, purpose, and goal.

Anyone who seeks an exact knowledge of the priesthood
and of its essential demands, can do nothing better than lift
his eyes to Christ and meditate reverently on our Lord's
personality. Such prayerful meditation will furnish him with
the clearest illumination and will most readily enable him
to realize what it means to become a priest. He will be
brought face to face with the prototype of all priesthood,
with the figure of Him in whom the ideal of priestly life and
labor has been perfectly realized. All other priests of the
past and present, no matter how great their holiness and
perfection, are after all only copies, only shadowy imitations
of the one infinitely great and holy High Priest who, in
the person of Christ, inaugurated the succession of New
Testament priests. Even the one who has long been a priest,
who for many years has borne the priestly dignity and the
priestly burden, must study our Lord in order to ascertain
whether and in what measure he has become another Christ
in his priestly life and labor.

Christ is the prototype and the gauge of all priesthood;
all priesthood in its essence is nothing else than a living
continuation and operation of Christ's high priesthood, a
participation in His vocation, a perpetuation of His mission.
Fundamentally there is in the New Testament economy of
salvation only one priesthood, the priesthood that Christ
Himself exercised and that He continues to exercise in a
spiritual manner through those who work in His person
and in His name as His priestly representatives.

2. The next question that arises concerns the purpose of Christ's vocation and mission. What did our Lord strive after while on earth and what did He accomplish? The answer to this question will give us a concrete picture of the mission and essence of the priesthood, and of the tasks and purposes that are proper to this vocation.

We know who Christ was. We know why the eternal, divine Logos became man, what He purposed to do on earth as God-man, what His teaching was, and what He accomplished. He came down from heaven for our sake, *propter nos homines et propter nostram salutem,* to redeem us, to show us by word and example the way to eternal salvation. Against the somber background of sin and its resultant misery which oppressed all mankind, the coming of Christ was like the dawn of a new and better day. His work was to establish a new supernatural creation, a new order, a new kingdom in the world. But not a kingdom of this world. His kingdom was to be entirely supernatural. Having nothing in common with earthly kingdoms or with measures of violence, His kingdom was to be one of reconciliation and grace. Sin alone was the enemy against which this kingdom was set up; sin was to be conquered and dethroned, and the final aim of Christ's kingdom was and continues to be the eternal fellowship of man with God.

Christ on earth pursued no earthly goals or interests; He attempted to solve no political or economic problems. The purpose of His life and labor was high above all these things, entirely in the domain of the spirit, in the realm of the holy, far removed from all that is profane and earthly. He taught spiritual truths and the supernatural law of God. To reveal to men the most profound mysteries of God, to build up a marvelous world of faith, to announce the will of His Father as the new rule of life—all these things were characterized by Himself as His task and mission. And so He walked in the world of men and journeyed through the towns and villages of His native land, not however sent to and destined for them alone, but embracing with the breadth of His vision and the fulness of His blessing all peoples of all times.

Theology sums up Christ's entire labor for the salvation of men under three fundamental concepts when it treats of His threefold office as teacher, priest, and shepherd. He was the most sublime teacher of mankind, the one true High Priest embracing all priesthoods, and the divine shepherd and leader given to all men.

The culmination of His mission, however, was reached in His journey to the place of sacrifice. Fallen mankind was to be redeemed, not merely by the teaching of new truths or the promulgation of new laws, but by an eminently sacerdotal and heroic act, the sacrifice of Christ on the cross. If sacrifice and priesthood belong together, this union attained its most perfect fulfilment in our Lord. As High Priest of mankind, chosen as such by His heavenly Father and anointed by the Holy Spirit, He did not follow the practice of the outgoing priesthood of His people and choose a sacrifice or burnt offering with which to effect the redemption of the world. He dedicated Himself as the victim, offering His own flesh and blood on the altar of the cross as a sacrificial gift to His heavenly Father. The voluntary, bloody immolation of Himself on the cross constituted the drama of Golgotha; it was Christ's unique and greatest act.

The cross was a sacrifice of world-embracing significance

and infinite value, sufficient for the redemption of the entire human race; its effects go back to the beginning of mankind's history, and forward to the end of time. To be able to offer such a sacrifice, the sacrificing priest had needs be endowed with divine power, had to surpass infinitely all human ability. Such was in fullest measure true of this sacrificing Priest who approached the bloody altar of sacrifice as the representative of mankind, for He was clothed with the fulness of divinity itself. To outward seeming, He was a mortal man, breathing forth His soul on the wood of the cross; but in the essence of His being He was lifted high above all that is human. He was "God of God, light of light, ... consubstantial with the Father." Precisely because He was the eternal, consubstantial Son of the heavenly Father, precisely because divinity and humanity were inseparably united in the unity of His divine Person, He was able to offer up a sacrifice of absolute worth and infinite merit. He was a priest, anointed not with oil but with the power of the Holy Spirit and with the fulness of the Godhead.

2. THE ESSENTIAL TASKS OF THE PRIEST

1. The priest, like Christ, is first of all a teacher, an announcer of divine truth. The word of God is placed upon his lips. What he has to announce in his character as priest is not human knowledge or wisdom, much less subjective opinions and convictions, but the eternal, immutable deposit of revelation imparted to man by God Himself. This mission of announcing and explaining the word and law of God constitutes at all times and in all places one of the most important tasks of his vocation. He is sent to preach to high

and low, rich and poor, lettered and unlettered, the truths and mysteries of divine revelation, which the individual must accept with unquestioning faith if he hopes to attain eternal salvation. This mission of preaching the word of God is obviously a holy and responsible task. The Apostles recognized it as their primary duty and, lest they should be forced to neglect it unduly, they transferred the charitable works of the primitive Christian community to the shoulders of the deacons.[2]

The Lord, in calling Saul to the apostolate, designated him as a vessel of election, as the one who would carry His name before the Gentiles, and kings, and the children of Israel.[3] St. Paul, who declared himself the teacher of the Gentile world, in his later apostolic life stressed this duty of his again and again, and labored indefatigably to discharge it. We read also how impressively he exhorted his co-workers to the same labor: "Preach the word!" was the solemn admonition of the aging Apostle to his disciple Timothy.[4] Moreover, Christ Himself, when commissioning the Apostles, had said: "Go ye into the whole world and preach the Gospel to every creature." [5]

Of course, this mandate to teach was placed by the Lord in the first instance and immediately upon the Apostles and their successors in the episcopal office. Hence today also, the bishops are the divinely appointed incumbents of the teaching office in the Church, while the lower clergy exercise this ministry only at the command of the bishops and by

[2] Cf. Acts 6: 2 ff.
[3] Cf. Acts 9: 15.
[4] See II Tim. 4: 2.
[5] Mark 16: 15.

virtue of the mission they receive from them. This circumstance, however, does not alter the fact that, practically and in most cases, the simple priest is the one upon whom rests the obligation to preach the truths of faith. The pope and the bishops take a personal and direct part in the preaching of the word only on rare and extraordinary occasions. Ordinarily and as a rule the teacher of the people in matters of faith is the simple, unassuming priest. Whether he stands before little children to give them catechetical instruction and speaks to them in language adapted to their understanding, whether he addresses vast congregations as a gifted pulpit orator, whether he lectures as a theologian of solid learning and extensive research on the most profound mysteries of divine revelation and their relation to one another, or whether he exercises his holy office by means of the spoken or the written word, he is always the teacher of the same, immutable, divine truth. It is his personal obligation and the duty of his vocation to penetrate into the inexhaustible riches of divine revelation and thereby place himself in a position to impart, with pedagogic skill and psychological adaptability, the eternally constant and sublime treasure of faith, now in one form, now in another, according to special conditions and circumstances.

In addition to announcing the truths of dogmatic faith, the priest is also commissioned to preach the divine moral law. He is the herald of Christian morality, the one who must champion the justness of its claims and its validity. To him has been entrusted the guardianship of the ten commandments, which contain the unchanging will of God and form the basis of all natural morality. By virtue of his office, the priest is the announcer and the advocate of our Lord's sublime ethics, which elevated the moral teaching of the Old Testament to highest perfection.

What would happen to the whole moral order of the world if Church and priesthood did not exist, ready at all times to step in with unswerving resistance when passions and errors threaten to overthrow the very foundations of morality? Such a question is more than ever justified today, in view of the moral degeneration that has shamelessly manifested itself in communism and other destructive tendencies. It is not too much to assert that our entire Christian culture would lapse into terrible chaos and the whole civilized world would revert to barbarism, if priestly teachers and guardians of morality were to close eyes and lips and cease to champion courageously the rights and duties of the Christian moral order. Thanks be to God, the Church is on the alert, and a devoted clergy, loyal to Christ, stands at the call of the eminent teacher of faith and morals in the Chair of Peter, a teacher whose power for good is unequalled in the world.

This, therefore, is the lofty and grave duty of the priest: to recall to the consciences of men, with apostolic candor and without human respect, the eternal laws of God, to announce the sublime ethics of the Gospels which surpass all human moral systems, and to do all this by virtue of a divine mission and of divine authority.

2. A further great task, essentially connected with the priesthood, consists in the administration of the means of grace instituted by Christ, the seven sacraments. "Let a man so account of us as of the ministers of Christ and the dispens-

ers of the mysteries of God." [6] With these significant words St. Paul points to an essential function of priestly vocation. Drawn up into the near presence of God and equipped by Him with divine powers, the priest returns to the people to distribute supernatural treasures and graces through the sacraments. Healing and purifying, elevating and sanctifying, bearing heavenly gifts in his hands, he approaches the individual soul.

Even though not all the graces of salvation merited by Christ flow through the channels of the seven sacraments, even though rich and precious graces are granted to souls directly by God Himself without the mediation of priests and sacraments, it nevertheless remains true that the ordinary and normal mediation of grace takes place by way of the sacramental signs. In this normal economy of salvation, established by Christ, the priest is the divinely appointed mediator and dispenser, through whose hands the streams of grace flow. We merely mention in passing that two of the seven sacraments, confirmation and holy orders, are usually administered only by the bishop as the one enjoying the fulness of priestly power; that in case of necessity anyone can baptize; and that in the reception of the sacrament of matrimony the priest acts simply as the official witness for the Church, while the administration of the sacrament in this last instance is committed to the hands of the couple who are uniting themselves in wedlock. These special cases, however, do not change the fundamental fact that the priest by virtue of his office and vocation is the ordinary dispenser of sacramental graces.

[6] See I Cor. 4: 1.

The priest in baptism lays the first and permanent foundation of supernatural life in the soul of the individual, leading the child into the Church of Christ. His priestly hand guides the stream of water that cleanses the soul of original sin and, in the case of adults, also of actual sins; from priestly lips issue the words of regeneration that accompany the pouring of the water; his hand clothes the soul with the invisible but radiant garment of divine sonship. In this way the priest becomes the spiritual father of his flock and, like St. Paul, can say: "I have begotten you." [7] This realization not only makes the priest aware of the supernatural and eternal significance of the baptismal ceremony, but bestows on him a supernatural parental dignity, a *dignitas* and *potestas paterna* within the Church.

Then, the administration of the sacrament of penance devolves upon the priest. He and he alone has the authority and the power to absolve from sin and guilt in the name of God and break the chains that fetter man to hell and perdition. He alone is able to reopen the gates of salvation to a soul that has strayed, and to lead it back to peace with God and conscience. Here, as nowhere else, he acts not so much as the stern judge but rather as the merciful Samaritan, pouring oil and wine into bleeding wounds. To practice charity and kindness and pity, to console, to bless—all these things are his high duty. To the merciful judge in the confessional, sinful souls manifest their needs and miseries; to his eyes are revealed the hidden recesses of the heart into which no other eye penetrates; in short, the priest as confessor receives a confidence that is found nowhere else on earth. What a lofty and even humanly satisfying ministry

[7] *Ibid.*, 4: 15.

is exercised by the priest in the confessional! For this reason he easily forgets all the hardships and inconveniences which this part of his ministry naturally entails. Disregarding them all, his priestly heart spurs him on to labor with renewed love for souls, that he may save and win them to eternal bliss. The most intimate and delicate care of souls is exercised by the priest in the tribunal of penance. Here he views the deep and terrifying abysses of sin, at which his own soul recoils in horror; and he learns to know souls of such pure, noble, and unselfish disposition, of such perfection and holiness, that his own priestly heart is filled with reverent awe and gladness.

The priest and the Eucharist—this phrase embraces a new cycle of duties for the incumbent of the sacerdotal office. To the priest is entrusted nothing less than the real body of Christ, the *corpus Christi reale*. He is the consecrator, endowed with divine power, who changes bread and wine into the body and blood of the God-man. He is the one who carries in his hands the holy grail and brings the bread of life to the hungry souls of men. As the servant of the Holy Eucharist, he walks through the holy of holies of the New Law, in the immediate presence of God Himself. The most precious legacy left by the Son of God on earth and committed to the care of His Church is entrusted to the power, the protection, and the administration of the priest. Must not priestly lips tremble with awe whenever they pronounce the words of consecration! Must not the heart of a priest quiver with reverence whenever his hands reach out to take his hidden God from the silent tabernacle and bring Him to the souls of men!

Dispensing grace, the priest meets the child at the threshold of life. Dispensing grace, he accompanies the individual through all the years of his earthly pilgrimage. At the close of life, he stands beside the tired traveler who is preparing to enter eternal rest. Once again the priest pours over the dying person the Church's treasures of grace, administering the last anointing of consolation and grace, which makes dying easier and assures the departing soul of entry into heavenly glory. This again is another phase of his unique ministry. As a rule, the deathbed of a dying person is a lonely and forsaken place; most people fear it and flee the sight of it. The priest of God, however, has his privileged place at the bedside of the dying, to speed the parting soul on its journey to eternity with his mediation of graces and his prayers. At such a moment when, in his presence and to the accompaniment of his words of blessing, the passage of a soul from time to eternity takes place, the priest himself is once more reminded of the unique character and the supernatural purpose of his holy vocation. Why is he a priest? Why does he as a priest hasten to the side of the dying? Not for earthly reasons, but solely to save an immortal soul for God and heaven.

3. The zenith of his vocation is reached, however, when the priest stands at the altar. That moment in the morning when he says *Introibo ad altare Dei* ushers in the most sacred hour of his day's work. On the platform of the altar he stands in the fullest sense of the words as an *alter Christus* in whose name and person he offers the perpetual sacrifice of the New Law. At the consecration of every mass he performs a mystery that possesses a marvel and majesty which can be perfectly grasped by God alone. It is no empty phrase and no exaggeration when Hettinger assures his

seminarian, Timothy: "So the mass becomes the central idea, the focal point in which the entire spiritual life of the Church is gathered, and from which all power and all impulse to a higher life emanate—the priest at the altar stands in the center of the world." [8]

Priest and altar are united in an inseparable, mysterious relationship. We marvel at the manner in which Christian art of the past and present has, in a spirit of living faith, produced altars of surpassing beauty and grandeur; we are deeply moved when we contemplate how the devotion of the faithful covers the table of sacrifice with gold and precious stones. But after all, what is really the most sublime and beautiful ornamentation of an altar? Undoubtedly the simple priest who stands there and with his words calls down the living God to the place of sacrifice.

Where no priest exercises his holy office and furnishes this living link between God and men, church and altar are dead and barren things. Only when a priest ascends to the altar does the dead stone take on meaning and life; it is then no longer cold and lifeless stone, but is the holy mount which Moses once ascended to be in the immediate presence of God and speak with Him. The altar "is a Bethlehem to which the Son of God descends, and not even in the form of a lowly child; He wishes to veil His majesty entirely, to surrender Himself into the hands of His priest, to be invisible, to hide Himself under the appearances of bread. Here is Emmaus where He tarries amongst us and our hearts burn within us as He speaks to our souls, while His countenance is still veiled from us. Here is Golgotha where we stand with Mary and John beneath the cross. Here is Good

---

[8] *Timotheus* (1909), pp. 44 f.

Friday sorrow and Easter joy, for He is risen and now dies no more. Here heaven and earth meet; here the eternal sun of grace rises, sending its rays into the murky night of earthly life, transfiguring and deifying everything. The earth is no longer a vast grave sown with the bones of the millions who have gone before us. God dwells in it, and it has become a holy land." [9]

Yes, the morning journey of the priest of God to the altar of sacrifice is ever the holiest and most priestly act of his ministry. Nothing on earth can compare with him in consecration and dignity when he stands at the altar of God. To be a priest means to ascend to the altar of God, to go up to that lofty and radiant height; in its brilliance everything else pales.

4. Lastly, a word must be said about the priest as shepherd of souls. Much that has been touched upon above belongs in the field of pastoral labor, a phase of priestly work that is *ex professo* a part precisely of the secular priest's ministry. Just as his rôle in the renewal of Christ's sacrifice lifts the priest into the immediate presence of God, so his vocation as shepherd of souls leads him back again to men. Christ the Lord spoke of Himself with special emphasis as the good shepherd and illustrated in His person the qualities that a good shepherd of a spiritual flock must possess. He must know his own, and his own must know him. He must love his flock, care for them, lead them to green pastures, abide with them in all loyalty and, if need be, lay down his life for them. He must be utterly unlike the hireling, who does not know his sheep and who, abandoning

[9] *Op. cit.*, p. 49.

his flock in the hour of danger and need, gives it over to destruction.

This pastoral activity in the spiritual and moral guidance of the souls of men, this protection and direction of immortal souls, undoubtedly constitutes one of the most sublime labors of the priestly ministry. Its proper performance naturally presupposes a profound and supernatural appraisal of each individual soul. It demands of the priest an unswerving and living faith in the truth that each individual soul, created by the benevolence of God, redeemed by the precious blood of Christ, and destined for an eternity of bliss in heaven, possesses a value far surpassing anything earthly or material. On the basis of this faith a priestly heart burns with consuming love for souls, and this love gives inspiration and motivation, warmth and life, to all his pastoral activity.

Hence, to practice care of souls means, in the first place, to love the souls of men as Christ loved them, to guide and protect them as He did and as He desires. It means to shield souls from spiritual dangers, to bring them into the light of faith, to direct them on the way to virtue and holiness, to point out to them by word and example the road to eternal salvation. The care of souls means to aid Christ and the Holy Ghost save immortal souls from the eternal damnation of hell and to win them for heaven—truly a divine work, one worthy of God. "God will have all men to be saved, and to come to the knowledge of the truth." [10] In His eternal decrees almighty God could not have willed anything more advantageous for the souls of men. And the

[10] See I Tim. 2: 4.

priest is the one who is called upon to act as a co-worker of God, to exert all his energy that this redemptive will of the Creator with regard to the whole of mankind may be realized as completely as possible. In fact, all of good and beauty that one person can supply to another in the way of knowledge, science, culture, or art never approaches in value the supernatural benefits that the priestly guide brings to a soul. All institutions established by almighty God and His divine Son in heaven and on earth have, in the final analysis, nothing but the *salus animarum* as their goal.

The care of souls is, at the same time, the noblest service of God and of humanity. For the redemption and salvation of souls purchased by the death of the Son of God, the triune God desires to employ human co-operation. The Holy Spirit, the dispenser of graces, does not will to act alone and in an invisible manner in the work of guiding and sanctifying men by means of His grace; the divine economy of salvation has provided that men are to be led and served by men. Regarded in this light, the pastor of souls is in the strict sense of the words a co-worker of God, and his labor is rightly termed a divine work.

Personal care of souls comprises two elements, salvation of souls and direction of souls. Many souls that have strayed from the right path would never find their way back but would be delivered over to eternal ruin, if there were no shepherd to go out after them and lead them back to the flock. Labor of this kind, however, postulates a priestly heart anointed with ardent and self-sacrificing love for Christ and for mankind. The priest clearly must have nothing in common with sin; he must hate it and avoid it more than others do. But the sinner himself, the poor human being who has erred, must be loved with the love of the good shepherd who, leaving the ninety and nine in the desert, goes after the strayed sheep and joyfully carries it back to the flock.

The good shepherd of souls never loses heart, never despairs, even when his best efforts seem to meet with no response. He has frequent occasion to exercise a vast amount of patience, forbearance, and self-denial. The success of genuine pastoral activity, today as always, lies not in a resigned pessimism that recognizes on all sides only the evil things in the world, but in an optimism based on trust in God, an optimism that does not lose faith in man or confidence in the ultimate victory of the good and of grace.

In spite of all the hardships demanded by his vocation, the real pastor of souls does not lack spiritual consolations. He experiences unspeakable interior joy when, after wearisome effort, he at last succeeds in saving an unfortunate soul. Tears of contrition, love, and gratitude were shed not only by Mary Magdalen at the feet of the Lord; they are frequently shed today at the feet of the priest.

Not every man is adapted by nature to lavish upon others the love and devotion that are required in pastoral labor. He who is engaged in the ministry must bring along *ab initio* a supernatural love for mankind, an apostolic zeal for souls, as precious gifts of nature and grace. Precisely from the soil of such a good natural disposition the seed of priestly vocation often sprouts, whereas colder natures, natures lacking the warmth of love from the start, rarely feel an inclination to the priesthood and, if they have chosen this vocation in spite of such a lack, find themselves little satisfied or happy therein.

Furthermore, care of souls implies the direction and guidance of souls. To guide with discerning hand and under the assistance of divine grace such souls as are in deadly earnest about climbing the heights of virtue and holiness, and to furnish them with solid spiritual sustenance, is a noble and eminently priestly duty. Souls of this kind are found on every side, even in our corrupt and godless times; souls that are touched by the breath of God and that nourish a burning desire to practice perfect imitation of Christ in the world or in the religious state. They seek in the priest, to whom they humbly commit themselves and whom they obey as the representative of God, a counselor and guide whose office it is to help them advance along the path of virtue. What a pastoral joy for the priest, what a consolation in the midst of the many disillusionments and vexations of his ministry, when a pure and holy life, a life dedicated to God in virtue, blossoms under his guiding hand! Such an experience more than compensates the priest for the bitter trials that are prepared for him in other quarters.

As if reflected in a mirror, the nature and unique character, the tasks and goals of the priesthood in their most important phases, have passed in review before our eyes. All secondary considerations were left to one side. Our sole purpose has been to determine what essentially pertains to the priest as such and to his ministry. God has not given to every man an understanding of this vocation or the inclination to dedicate himself to it and become in life and work another Christ in this complete sense of the phrase. On the other hand, we can easily appreciate how a high-minded boy, wishing to rise above the dust of earth and pursue the ideal, will feel himself strongly drawn to the priesthood, and heed the admonition of Christ: "Follow me." [11]

3. THE SUPERNATURAL CHARACTER OF THE PRIEST

Something very profound remains to be said. In view of the lofty and holy vocational tasks that a priest must discharge, the question spontaneously suggests itself: How can the priest, who after all is only a man, be equal to such tasks and such goals?

We can recognize that this question refers not merely to the supernatural equipment which every priest receives in ordination, but directly to the essence of his priestly character, to that element in the make-up of a priest that we have already called his mystical similarity, his essential analogy with Christ.

The same question arose with regard to our Lord. By what title and by what power was He able to do those works that aroused the amazement of the onlookers? What was at the root of His personality? The only true and adequate answer to these questions is that Christ was a superman, the God-man, that is, He was God and man in the unity of the second divine Person. In other words, He had a double nature; a divine nature that was proper to Him from all eternity and that made Him consubstantial with His heavenly Father, and a human nature that He had assumed in time from the Blessed Virgin Mary. These two natures were indissolubly united in the eternal Logos, and indeed in such a way that each preserved its own characteristics and modes

[11] Luke 5: 27.

of operation. The humanity of Christ was elevated to the heights and majesty of His divinity; or, as St. Paul viewing the matter from the opposite angle phrases it, the divinity of Christ descended to His humanity and the fulness of the Godhead dwelt in Him corporeally.[12]

Such is the dogmatic explanation of the fact that the words and actions of our Lord, human *in se* and performed by the natural organs of His body, acquired a superhuman and a supernatural, an eternal and a divine, power. The consecration and unction imparted by the divine essence itself gave to all the works of Christ their sublime worth. No ordinary or mortal man operated in and through Him, but a divine Person, an omnipotent Being, who used the human nature as His visible tool.

The priest, of course, does not possess such a double nature. He is and remains merely a man, even after he has attained the highest hierarchical rank. Holy orders do not confer upon him a higher or superhuman nature, but he does receive something similar to a higher nature, namely, supernatural dignity and divine power. As theology teaches, he receives both in such a manner that they are impressed upon his soul forever in the form of a *character indelibilis*. Once a priest, he remains a priest for all eternity. By sacramental consecration he is lifted out of the purely natural and earthly sphere, placed on a higher plane, and moved into the near presence of God, so that he becomes what St. Paul with full justice calls a "man of God." [13] In the last analysis, he receives his supernatural endowment and his mission, not from the bishop who imposes hands upon him,

[12] Cf. Col. 2: 9.
[13] See I Tim. 6: 11.

but from God Himself, in whose name the bishop acts. Just as the Blessed Virgin, in the moment when she became the mother of God, was touched by the grace of the Holy Spirit and overshadowed by the power of the Most High,[14] so also is the priest in the moment of his ordination, with the result that everything he says and does henceforth is, by virtue of the divine power he has received, a form of divine operation. "Who can forgive sins but God only?" [15] This fundamental principle to which the Pharisees appealed in order to accuse our Lord of blasphemy, when He actually dared to forgive sins, is absolutely true. When the priest forgives sins today, he is able to do so not of himself but only by virtue of the divine authority and competence with which he is endowed and with which he acts. God Himself speaks through his lips.

This truth is brought home to us even more graphically when we consider the words of consecration which the priest pronounces over the bread and wine. Viewed in the clear light of faith, we are here confronted with an action that only the God-man, on the basis of His essence, is empowered to perform, and that a human priest is able to accomplish only because something of the divine power of Christ is his.

Hence there really exists an analogy of essence between Christ and the priest, a constitutional similarity between them. Just as Christ is constituted of divinity and humanity, so the priest is constituted of his own humanity and the divine plenitude of power; this power, however, belongs to him not as a second nature added to his human nature, but as a divine quality that is inseparably united to his

[14] Cf. Luke 1: 35.
[15] Mark 2: 7.

human nature. Viewed from this ontological standpoint, the priest stands in the world as an *alter Christus,* as a kind of second God-man, as a being composed of the divine and the human, as a man of God in essence and nature.

On this analogy of essence is based the above-mentioned vocational analogy between Christ and the priest. As in his higher state of being, so also in his activity the priest is nothing else and nothing less than another Christ. The Catholic priesthood can be and wishes to be merely the perpetual continuation of the mission and life work of Christ. Only in this way can this institution be understood, only in this way can its origin and purpose be grasped. We have been led back to the first source, to Christ Himself. He is the divine Founder and also the sublime and essential content of the priesthood. *Sacerdos alter Christus.*

CHAPTER III

The Sublime Dignity
of the Priesthood

I. SOURCE AND ESSENCE

FUNDAMENTALLY the subject matter of this chapter is simply the logical conclusion drawn from the two preceding chapters. In the first chapter we spoke of the divine origin of priesthood as the direct creation of Jesus Christ, the Son of God. The second chapter dealt with the essence and mission of this state in life, and there again, the close connection between Christ and the priest was made evident. The relationship with Christ, thus far described, is the source from which all priestly dignity and greatness spontaneously flow. A state so intimately and indissolubly united with Christ must be called sublime and holy in its essence.

For us to become fully aware of the sublimity of the priesthood, it would perhaps suffice if, in a spirit of prayerful meditation, we were to review the thoughts already suggested. However, without repeating what has been said, we will endeavor to single out and place in a clearer light several outstanding characteristics of the priesthood, thus permitting the dignity of this vocation to shine forth in all its splendor. Our procedure will be one of calm and objective theological reflection; at the end we will mention some of the enthusiastic eulogies of the fathers and of later theologians.

It should hardly be necessary to state explicitly that we are here concerned only with the objective dignity and holiness of the priesthood, not with the subjective holiness of the individual priest or of the clergy as a whole, even though the objective dignity of this state naturally presupposes a corresponding subjective virtue on the part of the individual priests.

The objective grandeur and sublimity inherent in the Catholic priesthood can best be summed up under three main headings: participation in the priesthood of Christ, power over the real body of Christ, and power over the mystical body of Christ. The meaning of these familiar theological concepts will become evident to us in the course of the following treatment. Meanwhile, for a general understanding of the twofold power referred to, we merely remark that the former designates particularly the power of consecrating, that is, the power of celebrating the holy sacrifice of the mass. This consecratory power is also called the power of orders (*potestas ordinis*). By the second power, which has to do with the care and guidance of Christ's mystical body, the Church, we mean in general the power of jurisdiction, and in particular the power of absolving from sins. The Roman Catechism has defined the *potestas jurisdictionis* concisely in the following words: "To it pertain the government and direction of Christians and their guidance to the everlasting blessedness of heaven." [1]

---

[1] *Cat. Rom.*, II, cap. 7, q. 6. The Roman Catechism, departing from the usual interpretation, makes the power of absolution part of the *potestas ordinis*, not of the *potestas jurisdictionis*.

We do not assert, of course, that these three viewpoints comprise everything that constitutes the objective worth and sublime dignity of the priesthood. Much more could be added. But we rightly say that these three aspects are the most important and that, in greater or lesser degree, they contain everything else that contributes to the unparalleled excellence of this vocation.

2. PARTICIPATION IN THE PRIESTHOOD OF CHRIST

1. In the New Testament economy of salvation we have only one priesthood, just as we have only one sacrifice and, in the last analysis, only one priest. Christ the Son of God is this priest; He is priest par excellence, priest from the very first moment of His existence as God-man, anointed not with the oil of earth but with the power of the Holy Spirit, so that the fulness of the Godhead dwells in Him corporeally.[2] He is at the same time priest and victim. Not under the compulsion of men, but in voluntary surrender, He offered Himself in a bloody manner to His heavenly Father for the redemption of mankind. His death on the cross was a real sacrifice, a sacrifice of infinite worth, a perfect sacrifice of reparation and atonement, an unexcelled sacrifice of praise and thanksgiving, a sacrifice in every way worthy of the infinite majesty of His Father.

Christ, however, was called to be an eternal priest, and His sacrifice was to be perpetual. *Tu es sacerdos in aeternum.* "Thou are a priest forever according to the order of Melchisedech." [3] This prophetic word demanded fulfilment,

[2] Col. 2: 9.
[3] Ps. 109: 4.

not as if the bloody sacrifice of Christ had been insufficient, not as if, humanly speaking, an outraged God had not been appeased by the blood of His only Son, once shed. Precisely because the cross was an absolutely perfect sacrifice, it was not to be repeated; no other sacrifice was to have a place beside it. But the divine plan of salvation made provision that this one perfect sacrifice be renewed at all times and in all places on earth, for a perpetual remembrance and also that all mankind might be permitted to share in its fruits.

The re-enactment and renewal of the sacrifice of the cross occurs in the holy sacrifice of the mass. What took place in bloody form on the wood of the cross takes place in an unbloody manner on the table of the altar. But this difference in the manner of offering is only of secondary importance. In both places everything essential is the same. Christ Himself is the sacrificial gift and the sacrificing priest in each case. On the cross He acted in His own person; at holy mass He employs the agency of His priest.

In this eminently sacerdotal action the participation of the New Testament priesthood in the priesthood of the Son of God shines forth in its full splendor. The priest at mass is the representative of Christ. He is even more than that; standing at the altar, he acts *in persona Christi*. At the consecration, the most essential part of the Eucharistic sacrifice, he speaks wholly in the name and in the person of Christ; he speaks as Christ Himself. He does not say: This is the body of Christ, this is the blood of Christ, but explicitly: This is my body, this is my blood.

This mystical identification of the sacrificing priest with Christ enhances the former's participation in our Lord's priesthood to the highest degree. The individual priest at the altar does not perform a personal action; in its essence his act is an *actio Christi;* it is a renewal and a re-enactment of the highest and holiest act of Christ's life, His atoning sacrifice.

In view of this fact, St. John Chrysostom says: "For when thou seest the Lord sacrificed, and laid upon the altar, and the priest standing and praying over the victim, and all the worshipers empurpled with that precious blood, canst thou then think that thou art still amongst men, and standing upon the earth? Art thou not, on the contrary, straightway translated to heaven?" [4] In another place the same father of the Church, speaking of the holy sacrifice of the mass, says: "The works set before us are not of man's power. He that then did these things at that supper, this same now also works them. We occupy the place of servants. He who sanctifieth and changeth them is the same." [5]

2. What is true of the celebration of mass applies also to the administration of the sacraments by which the graces of the redemption are made accessible to men. Here also, the participation of the priest in the priesthood of Christ manifests itself, since all the sacraments are dispensed at the command of Christ and in His name; they receive their power and efficacy only through Him. Here also, it is Christ who cleanses and sanctifies the souls of men by means of the words and actions of the priest. To use the language of Scholastic theology, in the administration of the sacraments Christ is the *causa efficiens principalis,* that is, the efficient

---

[4] *De sacer.,* I, 3, cap. 4 (*PG,* XLVIII, 642). The wording of this quotation, as also of many other passages from the Church fathers cited in the course of this work, is taken from *A Select Library of the Nicene and Post-Nicene Fathers,* published by Charles Scribner's Sons.

[5] *Hom. 82 in Matt.* 26: 26–28 (*PG,* LVIII, 744).

cause from whom all power goes forth, while the priest is only the *causa instrumentalis,* the living instrument in the hands of Christ. St. Paul had occasion to bring this dogmatic truth home to the Christians of Corinth, when the Church of that place was split in contending factions: "What then is Apollo, and what is Paul? The ministers of him whom you have believed; and to everyone as the Lord hath given." [6] This parity between Christ and the priest in regard to the administration of the sacraments is stated in the clearest possible way also by St. Augustine: "Peter may baptize, but this is He [Christ] that baptizeth; Paul may baptize, yet this is He that baptizeth; Judas may baptize, still this is He that baptizeth." [7] By citing the name of Judas, St. Augustine meant to indicate in an impressive manner that the effect of the sacraments administered by Christ is not impaired by the moral unworthiness of the minister.

So closely are Christ and the priest joined to each other that they constitute not only one moral person but a living unit.[8] There can be no Catholic priesthood without the priesthood of Christ and, in the present order of things, the priesthood of Christ without the Catholic priesthood is simply impossible and inoperative. Because the Catholic priesthood presents such a close and living connection with the priestly office of Christ, it partakes of the objective holiness and the sublime dignity which our Lord, the divinely sent High Priest, united in His person. The logical conclusion, that His successors in the priesthood also have the duty of personal sanctification, is self-evident. We merely mention it here in

[6] See I Cor. 3: 5 f.
[7] *In Joan.* tract. 6, n.7 (*PL,* XXXV, 1428).
[8] Cf. Lohmann, *Ueber den Priesterstand* (1899), pp. 11, 13.

passing and will return to it for fuller treatment in a later chapter.

3. POWER OVER THE REAL BODY OF CHRIST

1. A second essential characteristic that belongs inseparably to the priesthood of the New Testament and that points to the zenith of its supernatural grandeur is the power over the real body of Christ (*potestas in corpus Christi verum sive reale*), in other words, the power of consecrating. Each time the priest exercises this specifically sacerdotal power, he stands at the high point, at the apex, of his vocation and his supernatural eminence. We have spoken at length in an earlier place of the priest at the altar, of the priest as the celebrant of the holy sacrifice of the mass. At this point we need merely to bring into clearer focus the central part of the mass, the consecration.

In conferring the holy order of priesthood, the bishop says to the deacon kneeling before him: "Receive power to offer sacrifice to God and to celebrate mass, as well for the living as for the dead," [9] thereby conferring upon the candidate the sublime fulness of power over the body of Christ, over Christ in His entirety. To acquire a feeble idea of the magnitude and extent of this power, we must again ascend to the mystical heights of dogmatic theology and see the real and living Christ present in the Holy Eucharist in all His fulness, body and blood, soul and divinity.

In a certain sense, the Eucharistic Son of God is committed to the hands of the priest more completely and more unreservedly than He was once committed in human form to the power and care of His virgin mother. When Mary said

[9] *Pontificale Romanum, de ordine presbyteri.*

to the angel: "Behold the handmaid of the Lord; be it done to me according to thy word," [10] the eternal Logos entered her pure womb to take unto Himself flesh and become man. Beside the fiat of Mary stand the words of the priest: *Hoc est corpus meum, hic est sanguis meus,* words of like significance and power. Mary's words and the words of the priest at mass constitute the begining of a divine life. Mary's words marked the beginning of the life of Christ in human form as the God-man; each time the priest utters the words of consecration they mark the beginning of the Eucharistic life of Christ under the sacramental species of bread and wine.

The words of consecration provide the Son of God with a new and altogether unique form of existence, the sacramental form. Per se, such a mode of existence fits only a purely spiritual being, and divine omnipotence alone can make it possible for a material being or a human body.[11]

Theology recognizes in the Son of God a threefold mode of existence. He receives His eternal divine being from the bosom of His heavenly Father. In time, He received His mode of existence as God-man through the operation of the Holy Ghost in the virginal womb of Mary, a form of existence in which He was visible to men during His sojourn of earth and which He now continues in a glorified state at the right hand of God. He regularly assumes His third form of existence, the sacramental, at the consecration of bread and wine; and this last mode of existence depends directly upon the words of the priest.

The sacramental or Eucharistic presence of Christ is rightly called a miracle of divine omnipotence, wisdom, and love.

[10] Luke 1: 38.
[11] Cf. Lohmann, *op. cit.,* p. 16.

That it does not arouse the wondering astonishment of men is due simply to the circumstance that it takes place in a manner entirely hidden and that it is not perceptible to the senses. Reason, even when illumined by faith, is able to grasp only vaguely and darkly the intrinsic possibility of this marvel; it can never comprehend it completely. The sacramentally present Christ is the richest and most profound mystery at the disposal of the Church in her mediation of grace and in her liturgy; it is the brightest jewel that mankind as a whole possesses on earth; it resembles an eternal fountain from which the streams of grace gush forth in torrential abundance. What would the mightiest cathedrals and the most splendid altars and all the magnificence of ecclesiastical art and liturgy amount to, if no sacramental Son of God were present to give these things of beauty their significance? And the priest—how great and sublime he appears, since he is the one whose lips pronounce the words that bring about the sacramental presence of the Son of God! To a believing soul the most majestic temple seems barren and cold, empty and dead, when no priest exercises his priestly office within its walls, when the Eucharistic God, the *Deus absconditus*,[12] has vanished from its tabernacle.

Theological speculation may ask which of the two is more potent and effective: the fiat of Mary or the words of consecration spoken by the humblest priest. In a certain sense, undoubtedly the latter. The fiat of the Blessed Virgin simply expressed her acquiescence in the decree of God and her consent to the operation of the Holy Spirit within her; she herself was only the passive instrument which the power of the Most High used at the incarnation of the Logos. The

[12] Is. 45: 15.

words of consecration, on the other hand, signify more. They carry with them some of the creative omnipotence of God, since by them the change of substance is causally effected and the Son of God actively endowed with new existence and life. To avoid misunderstanding, we must refer again in this place to what has been said before, namely, that the consecrating priest serves only as the instrumental cause, while Christ Himself is the real efficient cause. But even this distinction does not alter the remarkable fact that the priest of God is the one who brings the mystery to pass.

And something else must be added. Mary the mother of God spoke her fiat only once. The priest, however, utters the words of consecration again and again, and always with the same sublime effect, in each instance providing the Son of God with His sacramental existence anew.

This control over the Eucharistic Christ is the acme, the burning focal point of priestly power and dignity. The Blessed Sacrament is the same divine Son whose might and majesty are described with such vivid imagery in the Scriptures; the same Jesus who said of Himself that He had been given all power in heaven and in earth;[13] the same Christ of whom St. Paul bore testimony "that in the name of Jesus every knee should bow, of those that are in heaven, on earth, and under the earth."[14]

Far from being idle and purposeless, it is salutary that the individual upon whom such power and dignity have been conferred advert to them often and with reverence. In this way a priest will most fully realize the essence and nature of his priesthood; he will more adequately comprehend what

[13] Matt. 28: 18.
[14] Phil. 2: 10.

it means for him personally to be a priest. Those who are not yet priests, but who are preparing for the reception of that high office, may well meditate earnestly upon the words of the last provincial synod of Cologne (1860): "The Church, having in mind the great dignity of the priesthood, most ardently desires that those who aspire to this office be seriously concerned about ordering all their efforts and their entire way of life in accordance with the requirements of such a high dignity." [15]

4. POWER OVER THE MYSTICAL BODY OF CHRIST

We must now treat in some detail the third basic reason for the superlative eminence of the priestly dignity. Theologians call it the *potestas in corpus Christi mysticum*. What does this expression mean?

1. Theology distinguishes between the *corpus Christi reale*, of which we have just spoken, and the *corpus Christi mysticum*. This moral or mystical body of Christ is the Church as the supernatural congregation of all the faithful. The conception of the Church as the mystical body of Christ goes back to St. Paul, who introduced this idea into Christian thought.

The congregation of all the faithful and also the individual Christian community appeared to St. Paul as a living spiritual organism with head and members, with "joints and bands, being supplied with nourishment and compacted," [16] an organism which, like the body, receives all life and power and movement from the head. Christ is the head of this

[15] *Acta et decreta Conc. Prov. Coloniensis* (1862), p. 135.
[16] Col. 2: 19.

mystical body, the Church, and the faithful are the members. "And he [Christ] is the head of the body, the Church," [17] "the head from which the whole body, . . . groweth unto the increase of God." [18] That this body must develop and conform inwardly to the image of God is a thought which St. Paul stresses with special emphasis. He admonishes the Christian community at Ephesus to hold itself aloof in every respect from deception and error, and "in all things grow up in him who is the head, even Christ." To establish his thesis, he continues: "From whom [Christ] the whole body, being compacted and fitly joined together, by what every joint supplieth, according to the operation in the measure of every part, maketh increase of the body, unto the edifying of itself in charity." [19]

What the Apostle seeks to express by means of this figurative language is quite evident. The profound meaning of his words is simply that the faithful, both among themselves and also with relation to Christ, are joined by invisible bands into a living community growing up toward God, and indeed in such a way that Christ is the creative and life-giving head of this organic community. Very aptly Karl Adam writes: "Christ the Lord is the real self of the Church. The Church is the body permeated through and through by the redemptive might of Jesus." [20]

In the last analysis, however, the Pauline conception of the Church goes back, in essence if not in specific symbolism, to Christ Himself. While St. Paul employs the picture of the head and members of a living body, Jesus uses the parable

[17] *Ibid.*, 1: 18.
[18] *Ibid.*, 2: 19.
[19] Eph. 4: 15 f.
[20] *The Spirit of Catholicism* (1929), p. 15.

of the vine and its branches to illustrate the same thought. "I am the vine; you the branches: he that abideth in me, and I in him, the same beareth much fruit: for without me you can do nothing." [21] By means of this parable Christ also wished to illustrate and emphasize the truth that between Him and the individual soul there exists a fruitful and living relationship which may not be wantonly destroyed without imperiling the attainment of salvation.

Grace is the term we use to express the idea of this fruitful life that goes out from Christ and flows in superabundance to the individual members of His Church.[22] The divine and holy influence of grace permeates the Church, furnishing it with life, growth, and the richest fecundity. The primary source and the dispenser of this spiritual gift of God is Christ Himself, since by His atoning death He has merited all graces and applies them to men through the operation of the priesthood which He has instituted.

2. From this last fact, the fundamental importance of the priesthood within the Church (the mystical community of Christ) becomes at once manifest. Just as the Eucharistic body of Christ is entrusted entirely to the hands of the priest, so in like manner is also the mystical body of Christ, the congregation of all the faithful. Over this body, too, the priest is granted plenary power; to him are entrusted the life and growth, the care and nurture of the *corpus mysticum*. Even though not all graces flow through priestly hands, still, as the ordinary minister of the sacraments, he is also the ordinary mediator of grace, especially of sanctifying grace.

The priest is the one through whose sacramental action

[21] John 15: 5.
[22] Cf. John 10: 10.

Christ achieves His mysterious and salutary effects in the souls of men. By means of the sacrament of baptism, the priest has the duty of laying the foundation for the individual's community of life with Christ. Each time he baptizes, he establishes anew the mystical kingdom of God. The priest ushers the individual into the Church and opens to him the fonts of grace that flow in such rich abundance through the kingdom of Christ on earth.

Again, it is the priest who has the privilege, the power, and the duty of supplying the members of Christ's body with the supernatural nourishment necessary for their supernatural life. With juice pressed from the grape and changed by his word into the blood of Christ he strengthens the single branches that are united to the heavenly vine. With bread produced by the earth and altered by him into the body of Christ, he feeds the individual members of the *corpus mysticum*. In very truth, the mystical, as well as the Eucharistic, body of Christ is committed to the care of the priest.

The priest is the one empowered to breathe new life into such members of Christ's body as have died through sin. For he, and he alone, possesses power to forgive sins in the name of God. The words, *Ego te absolvo a peccatis tuis,* which he pronounces over the penitent sinner, have a sin-deleting and a life-giving power. The priest, in truth, goes among the people of God on earth as the dispenser of divine life and the bearer of supernatural power; he looses and binds with an effect that has validity for God and heaven.

Further, it is the priest who, like an anxious physician, is greatly concerned about those members of the mystical body who are afflicted with bodily sickness; anointing them with oil and fortifying them with the powerful grace of Christ, he makes them ready for the journey to eternity. At the end, the priest is the one who consigns the mortal remains of the departed member to the bosom of consecrated earth and pronounces over the grave the blessing of the Church.

In this manner does the consecrated priest discharge his holy duties toward the mystical body of Christ. The sublime authority over this body, an authority which he has received from God, becomes for him a duty and an office that burden him with the gravest responsibility. "Woe is unto me," cries St. Paul, "if I preach not the Gospel." [23] Outwardly and in the eyes of the world, this august power with which the priest of God, his hands overflowing with graces, accompanies men from the cradle to the grave, may be little in evidence, but this circumstance does not rob it of any of its importance and sublimity.

5. PASSAGES FROM THE CHURCH FATHERS AND LATER THEOLOGIANS

To recognize and appreciate the unique significance and the sublime power of the Catholic priesthood, we must be able to see with the eye of faith and to judge values from the standpoint of the supernatural and the eternal. People who take their stand exclusively on the basis of nature, who recognize only palpable and material values, whose vision does not penetrate into the world of supernature with its mysteries and its miracles, will not be able to summon up any understanding for the greatness of an institution like the Catholic priesthood. For them the supernatural and divine character of the Church, even of Christianity in general, remains an

[23] See I Cor. 9: 16.

incomprehensible and puzzling phenomenon. They barely see its external side; they never penetrate to its essential nature.

On the other hand, men of the spirit, men who were gifted with more penetrating vision, men whose minds were supernaturally enlightened and who tried in a spirit of lofty mystical contemplation to grasp the essence and sublimity of the priesthood, found no words or expressions adequate to convey what they had seen and experienced with the eye and heart of faith. The dithyrambic effusions and the poetic flights of fancy with which the fathers of antiquity, in particular, glorified and extolled the priesthood may indeed strike the ears of an unbelieving worldling as the fantastic product of a diseased imagination; actually they are only the weak expression of a true appreciation of the priestly ideal in all its beauty and grandeur, and an attempt to clothe this conviction in the imperfect garb of human speech. As a matter of fact, it would be necessary to speak the tongue of angels rather than the language of men, in order to do full justice to the sublimity of the priesthood. Measured by the reality, the enthusiastic language with which the Church fathers spoke of the power and dignity of the priesthood resembles the feeble stammering of a child. The same is true of the forms of expression used by the Church in many councils to extol the grandeur of this state.

The following excerpts, taken from the panegyrics that come as a mighty hymn of praise from the lips of the fathers and later enthusiastic theologians, are to be so understood. We will have to content ourselves with singling out merely a few of the many voices in the great chorus that greets us. But they are voices that betray a fervent emotion of the heart as well as a most profound conviction of the mind. Even sober theological reflection will not succeed in taking from these expressions of spellbound wonder their factual justification.

To illustrate at once, by means of a striking example, the lofty sublimity of thought that characterized the fathers when they dealt with the subject of the priesthood, we place at the beginning of this section a literal translation of the hymn of praise composed by the "harp of the Holy Spirit," St. Ephraem (d. 373):

O extraordinary marvel, O unspeakable power, O awe-inspiring mystery of the priesthood! O spiritual, sacred, august, and blameless office that Christ after His coming left to us unworthy ones! I cast myself down and beg with tears and sighs that we may consider what a treasure the priesthood is for those who guard it in a worthy and holy manner. It is a shining and incomparable shield, an unshakable tower, an indestructible wall. It is a solidly built edifice towering up from the earth to the vault of heaven. But what am I saying, brethren? It reaches up to the highest vault of heaven. It penetrates unchecked into the very heaven of heavens; shining and radiant in the midst of the angels, it walks with the bodiless spirits. But what am I saying? With the powers above? Aye, it cultivates familar intercourse with the Lord of angels Himself and approaches Him at pleasure with complete confidence. . . . Through the priesthood the world acquires salvation, creation receives light; through it the mountains and hills and valleys and caves are filled with a blessed generation, namely, that of the monks. . . . Through it lawlessness has been banished from the world, and discipline now reigns on earth. Through it the devil has been overthrown, and his power destroyed, the dissolute have become holy vessels, the impure clean and spotless, the unwise have become leaders toward justice, and the ruthless have become holy and godly. Through it, moreover, the power of death has been broken, hell has lost its might, the curse placed upon Adam has been lifted, and the heavenly bridal chamber prepared. Through it the nature of man is transformed into the might of the bodiless.[24]

Without doubt, we are here listening to a poet, on fire for the things of God, drawing upon his rich poetic fancy for pictures and expressions to describe the nature and salutary operation of the priesthood. Even though, upon critical examination, the cold reality many seem to remain far behind the ideal of the priesthood and especially of its salutary operation, sketched by the gifted poet and orator with such rapture, the substance of his thought nevertheless remains true: the priesthood is the loftiest and the holiest state that we can conceive of on earth.

Passing on to another patristic testimony, we find that St. John Chrysostom (d. 407) has spoken of the priesthood in like manner and in his own eloquent style. To him this state "exceeds a kingdom as much as the spirit differs from the flesh." [25] Continuing, this great Church father cries out in amazement and admiration:

These verily are they who are entrusted with the pangs of spiritual travail and the birth which comes through baptism: by their means we put on Christ, and are buried with the Son of God, and become members of that blessed Head. Wherefore they might not only be more justly feared by us than rulers and kings, but also be more honored than parents; since these begot us of blood and the will of the flesh, but the others are the authors of our birth from God, even that blessed regeneration which is the true freedom and the sonship according to grace.[26]

[24] *De sacerd.*, cap. 1 et 2 (Assemani, *Ephr. Syr. opera graece*, III, 1–2).
[25] *De sacerd.*, 1, 3, cap. 1 (*PG*, XLVIII, 641).
[26] *Loc. cit.*, cap. 6.

The comparison with earthly parents is further and more profoundly developed by the saint as follows:

The two [i. e., parents and priests] indeed differ as much as the present and the future life. For our natural parents generate us unto this life only, but the others unto that which is to come. And the former would not be able to avert death from their offspring, or to repel the assaults of disease; but these others have often saved a sick soul, or one which was on the point of perishing, procuring for some a milder chastisement, and preventing others from falling altogether, not only by instruction and admonition, but also by the assistance wrought through prayers.[27] ...
For they who inhabit the earth and make their abode there are entrusted with the administration of things which are in heaven, and have received an authority which God has not given to angels or archangels.[28] ... For the priestly office is indeed discharged on earth, but it ranks amongst heavenly ordinances; and very naturally so: for neither man, nor angel, nor archangel, nor any other created power, but the Paraclete Himself instituted this vocation, and persuaded men while still abiding in the flesh to represent the ministry of angels.[29] ... For they [the priests] have been conducted to this dignity as if they were already translated to heaven, and had transcended human nature, and were released from the passions to which we are liable.[30]

Such is the language of the most esteemed Church fathers concerning the sublime dignity of the priesthood. Their judgments on this subject are all the more significant because they have not remained the private opinions of the

[27] *Loc. cit.*
[28] *Loc. cit.*, cap. 5.
[29] *Loc. cit.*, cap. 4.
[30] *Loc. cit.*, cap. 5.

fathers; countless theologians and spiritual writers of later ages have made them their own; ecclesiastical synods and papal documents have incorporated them in their pronouncements, thus raising them to the status of a general opinion of the Church. Almost invariably and right down to our own day we find that the greater councils, whenever they busied themselves with the question of the dignity and holiness of the sacerdotal state, quoted one or the other of the above passages, thereby showing that the Church intended to make these utterances of the fathers her own.[31]

3. The theologians of the Roman Catechism and all the popes and bishops who sponsor and give authoritative standing to this classical textbook pass the same judgment. In the Catechism of the Council of Trent we read: "The priests of the New Testament far surpass all others in dignity; for the power, both to confect and to offer the body and blood of our Lord, and also to remit sins, which has been conferred upon them, surpasses all human reason and understanding; nor can anything like it or equal to it be found on earth." [32]

Of the power of the New Testament priesthood we read: "For this power is heavenly and surpasses even all the power of the angels; nor does it have its origin in the Mosaic priesthood, but in Christ the Lord who was priest not according to Aaron, but according to the order of Melchisedech." [33] Of the priests themselves the Catechism declares, in conclusion: "Segregated from the rest of the people, they exercise a ministry that is by far the greatest and most august of all." [34]

[31] Cf. *Acta et decreta Conc. Prov. Coloniensis* (1862), pp. 147 f.
[32] *Cat. Rom.*, II, cap. 7, q. 2.
[33] *Loc. cit.*, q. 8.
[34] *Loc. cit.*, q. 5.

When we ponder the full import of these and similar passages, we recognize at once that they coincide substantially with the hymns of praise chanted by the fathers. Priests are further described by the Catechism as the interpreters and heralds of God, as the ones who in God's name teach the divine law and rule of life, even as the ones who take God's place on earth. In truth, their office is so great that a greater cannot even be conceived, and the priests themselves rightly deserve to be called not only angels but gods.[35]

From these considerations the Roman Catechism draws the conclusion, which we will examine more at length in another place, that the holiness of the priestly office presupposes holiness in the individual priests, and that, in addition to knowledge and prudence, the primary and greatest emphasis must be placed upon the moral fitness of the candidates for the priesthood: "First of all, therefore, integrity of life and morals is of the greatest importance in him who is to be made a priest." [36]

Therefore these candidates must realize how incomprehensibly lofty and sublime are the power and dignity to which they are called. The sacerdotal power with which they are to be endowed reaches from earth to heaven, from time into eternity. What is the priest? *Nihil et omnia*—nothing of himself, but everything through God.

[35] *Loc. cit.*, q.2.
[36] *Loc. cit.*, q.16, 2.

CHAPTER IV

The Priesthood in the Light
of the New Testament

IN THE following commentary we obviously cannot attempt
to give, on the basis of the New Testament Scriptures, a complete picture of the essence, dignity, and mission of the
Catholic priesthood. Such an undertaking, no matter how
profitable in itself, would lead us far beyond the purpose and
scope of this treatise. We must limit ourselves, therefore, to
a consideration of the various typical characterizations of
priest and priesthood that came from the lips of our Lord
and His Apostles and are recorded in the books of the New
Testament. These utterances will help us to acquire a more
profound understanding of the meaning and purpose of
this sublime vocation. We are dealing here with descriptive
phrases that cast a searching light upon the unique character
of the priesthood, and they are the more significant because
they proceed from the most authoritative and competent
source. Surely, no one is in a position to pass a more accurate
or profound judgment upon the meaning and mission of the
priesthood than Jesus Christ Himself, the primary source
and founder of this vocation; and next to our Lord, who
could have had a better insight into the nature of the priesthood than the Apostles, the men He Himself trained to be
the first priests?

We intend to ponder prayerfully the pithy and authoritative sentences of our Lord Jesus and His Apostles concerning the priesthood, that they may produce their full effect upon our minds and hearts. To the meditative soul of a priest, even of one who has grown gray in the ministry, these words have a far more important message than may at first glance appear.

I. "SALT OF THE EARTH AND LIGHT OF THE WORLD"

"You are the salt of the earth. . . . You are the light of the world." [1] These majestic words, taken from the Sermon on the Mount and addressed by our Lord to the Apostles, contain no logically pointed definition of the office of priest and apostle, but they express, tersely, impressively, and in the garb of oriental imagery and parable, a most profound truth.

1. *Sal terrae*, salt of the earth. Everyone knows the importance of salt in nature and in the life of man. Vitally necessary for the living organism in the animal and vegetable kingdoms, it is also of vast importance in the domestic and economic life of man. The primary function of salt consists in preserving nature and organic life from decay and dissolution, and also in giving seasoning and relish to human food. It seems silly to say that Jesus, when He used this expression, thought of all the various chemical and physical effects of salt that present-day scientific research has brought to light. He was speaking to simple people in figurative language adapted to general understanding, and He intended to put into the metaphor of salt nothing more than the average person of His time could understand. But even that

[1] Matt. 5: 13, 14.

limited popular knowledge of the properties of salt was amply sufficient for His purpose.

What truth did He wish to illustrate by means of this figure? Simply that the Apostles and their successors were to be for mankind what salt is for nature in general. They, also, were to act as a preservative, safeguarding mankind from the moral decay of sin, permeating the souls of men with the power of the graces entrusted to their care, and thus preparing men for their eternal destiny. And in truth, the Catholic priesthood acts as a divine salt in the midst of mankind. Steadfastly it champions the eternal truths and the immutable moral law, untiringly it defends the interests of God on earth. What would become of religion and morality if no Catholic priesthood existed to guard these holiest possessions of mankind from profanation and corruption? A lofty and supremely sacred task has indeed been assigned to the priesthood.

The individual priest is the salt of the earth by means of the moral laws and the truths of faith which he proclaims in the name of Christ, by means of the graces which he administers, by means of his whole personality that is consecrated to the service of God and man and that, by its very presence in the world, calls to mind a higher and supernatural order. The priest himself will, of course, do more justice to this vital part of his mission, the more firmly he has established himself on the sublime heights of his vocation and the more he measures up, by the moral perfection of his life and person, to the standard of holiness demanded by his office. Hence, the metaphor used by our Lord contains, and not in last place, an admonition to the priest himself. Moreover, Jesus drove home this solemn warning in unmistakable terms when He added: "But if the salt lose its savor, wherewith shall it be salted? It is good for nothing any more but to be cast out, and to be trodden on by men." [2] No doubt, when He spoke these melancholy words, the Master's heart was heavy with sadness as he thought of those of His priests who, forgetful of their dignity and mission, would become as salt that has lost its savor and potency. And what of those unfortunates? The Lord's words are clear and terrifying. Woe to the unhappy priest who has ceased to be the salt of the earth!

2. *Lux mundi,* light of the world. These words contain another apt figure with which Christ illustrates the significance of the priestly office. For natural life, light is no less essential than salt. All life, of man, of animal, and of plant, yearns for the light of the sun. Life languishes and slowly perishes when light is withdrawn from it. The function of light is to give warmth, to dispel darkness, to shine, to illumine, to spread brightness before the eye. The Creator placed the giant orb of the sun in the firmament to provide light for the world. To man He gave the natural light of reason which enables him to penetrate into the boundless realm of truth; to the natural light of reason He has added the supernatural light of revelation and of faith, which opens up to mankind a higher world.

Christ spoke of Himself with impressive force as the light of the world. "I am the light of the world." [3] With these words He pointed to a sublime aspect of His Messianic vocation. He had come to enlighten the world with divine doctrines and supernatural truths, as He solemnly declared

[2] *Ibid.,* 5: 13.
[3] John 8: 12.

before Pilate: "For this was I born, and for this came I into the world, that I should give testimony to the truth." [4] Now, the light which He Himself was and which "enlighteneth every man that cometh into this world," [5] was to continue to shine in the person of His disciples and their successors in the priesthood, after the Master's departure. According to the will of the Lord, therefore, Apostles and bishops and priests are called to be light-bearers, carrying His light to the nations of the world and letting it shine wherever men are found. They are to be light-bearers by word and by example.

The eternal and unchangeable word of God that it is the priest's duty to announce has, today as always, the effect of a brilliant light emanating from a higher world, a light that reveals the errors of men and that alone can shed illumination upon the dark riddles of life. Time and again this light of faith has been a salutary beacon for men in search of the truth, leading them to the haven of certainty. For countless wavering souls it has been a guiding star, giving them their correct position and pointing out their true course.

The priesthood of the Catholic Church is without question a salutary light for the whole world, and through the centuries the Vatican in Rome, that exalted seat of the supreme pontiff, has increasingly proved itself to be the city seated on a mountain, a city that cannot be hid.[6] How the present-day world listens for every word coming from the *cathedra Petri!* In truth, a papal pronouncement has often had the effect of a liberating and clarifying light; its penetrating

[4] *Ibid.,* 18: 37.
[5] *Ibid.,* 1: 9.
[6] Matt. 5: 14.

rays have shone upon the errors of an unbelieving age and disclosed their falsity. If in our time, to cite a recent example, the intellectual system of naturalism and liberalism appears outmoded and inherently untenable, we can point with satisfaction to the fact that a Roman pontiff (Pope Pius IX) was the one who dared solemnly to condemn this system before the whole world, at a time when it was in full flower and held a dominating position in the intellectual field.

In a greater or lesser degree, every priest has a share in this light-dispensing activity which the Church exercises through her supreme teaching office. For the heavenly light that streams from Vatican Hill is carried by priests to the remotest villages and into the humblest dwelling places of men. Every priest, therefore, is by virtue of his office a "light of the world." This truth should fill him with an exalted appreciation of his vocation and should console even the priest in the most forsaken outpost by reminding him that he, as a disseminator of divine light, has in the last analysis more to give mankind than the worldly wise in their proud seats of learning.

Our present age is justifiably proud of the advances that science has made, and we are amazed at the marvelous creations of technical ingenuity. But if we turn our attention to the loftiest domain of culture, the sphere of religion and morality, who would dare assert that a corresponding advance has taken place there? Must we not rather admit that a lamentable regression is to be observed? In an age when the darkness of night is being dispelled by myriads of artificial lights, the flame of religion has been extinguished in all too many hearts. The most recent attempts to bring about the gradual disappearance of Christianity from public and private life and to hurl mankind back into the religious and moral darkness of ancient paganism have indubitably been making headway and gaining ground steadily. The philosophical slogan regarding the overthrow of all values has sown an accursed seed which has begun to germinate.

And who is the one that dares resolutely to combat this threatened collapse of the whole moral order and this attempt to plunge the world into spiritual darkness? Nobody else, or at least nobody more, than the Catholic priest. Today as heretofore, the priesthood holds aloft the flaming torch of truth, of the Gospel. Catholic priests are the ones who set the light "upon a candlestick, that it may shine to all that are in the house." [7]

2. "MAN OF GOD"

Homo Dei. The priest is a "man of God." This is the title given him by St. Paul in writing to his disciple Timothy: "For the desire of money is the root of all evils; which some coveting have erred from the faith, and have entangled themselves in many sorrows. But thou, O man of God, fly these things." [8]

Man of God. We have here an expression full of the deepest meaning, a phrase that designates, first of all, the essential union between the priest and God. A man of God is one who derives his origin from God; one who, as it were, is begotten of God; a man whose whole trend and aim in life are toward God; a man whose vocation it is to stand with undivided heart and in complete devotion on the side of God. All these things are certainly true of the priest. As

[7] *Ibid.,* 5: 15.
[8] See I Tim. 6: 10 f.

a priest, he does not trace his origin to himself, nor has he been so fashioned by men; he has come from God alone. The Lord called him to the sacerdotal state and, by means of sacramental consecration, placed him in His sanctuary. Every priest, therefore, is of God and also for God. He is obligated entirely to God. His vocation, which engages all his powers and his entire person, aims solely at representing the interests and promoting the plans of God among men, upholding and advancing the kingdom of God, bringing God's will into fulfilment on earth. In the exercise of his lofty calling he moves in a heavenly atmosphere. The layman, engaged in secular pursuits, comes into the religious sphere and into the near presence of God only incidentally and in connection with his spiritual needs and duties—no matter how often and how regularly this may occur. The priest stands there always and by virtue of his vocation. For his vocation is identical with religion, and his place of labor is always in the near presence of God.

The liturgical vesture of the Israelitic high priest included a plate of purest gold, on which were engraved the words: "Holy to the Lord." [9] This plate was tied with a violet fillet and attached to the miter in such a way that it hung over the high priest's forehead. Thus was made manifest to all the truth that this man was withdrawn from the sphere of profane life and dedicated entirely to God. In a far higher degree, the same applies to every New Testament priest, high and low. By virtue of the unction and consecration conferred upon him, by virtue of the office and the supernatural authority with which he has been invested, he has been lifted completely out of the earthly and profane sphere,

[9] Ex. 28: 36.

and placed in the religious and the sacred; in the fullest sense of the words, he is "holy to the Lord." For this reason the Church makes the aspirant to the priesthood, at the time of his acceptance into the clerical state, repeat and apply to himself the words of Holy Writ: "The Lord is the portion of my inheritance and of my cup: it is thou that wilt restore my inheritance to me." [10]

Hence the priest is a man of God, first of all, in the ontological order of supernature, as a result of the indelible character which the sacrament of holy orders impresses upon his soul. But he is expected to be even more than that. He must also be a man of God in the moral order. The holiness demanded by his vocation and his own personal moral life should fuse in perfect harmony, that is, he should strive to be inwardly what he appears to be outwardly and by virtue of his vocation. Therefore he may not be a man of the world; he may not, like the layman, be given to the pursuit of earthly and temporal interests, but his personal conduct and his whole way of life, his entire mode of thought, must be devoted to the spiritual, the sacred, the supernatural. To him in particular applies St. Paul's admonition: "And be not conformed to this world: but be reformed in the newness of your mind, that you may prove what is the good and the acceptable and the perfect will of God." [11] The consecrated man of God must be a spiritual man whose thoughts are directed on high, in contrast to the merely natural and carnal man who "perceiveth not these things that are of the Spirit of God." [12] His primary moral duty is "to put on the

10 Ps. 15: 5.
11 Rom. 12: 2.
12 See I Cor. 2: 14.

new man, who according to God is created in justice and holiness of truth." [13] Another sentence penned by the same great Apostle contains a program for every priest who is in earnest about becoming a *homo Dei*: "Pursue justice, godliness, faith, charity, patience, mildness. Fight the good fight of faith: lay hold on eternal life, whereunto thou art called." [14]

Precisely because the characteristic trait of the genuine man of God consists in this lofty direction of the spirit, we can easily understand why the Church is so concerned about the training of priestly candidates, why she strives to free them betimes from all secular inclinations and ways of thought, from all earthly and petty interests, and lead them step by step along the road of self-denial and personal sanctification into the loftier region of the spirit.

In spite of the great love for mankind and the pastoral concern for the world that are essential equipment for the pastor of souls in our day, the genuine priestly heart must nevertheless give evidence of an inner aloofness, of a deliberate and conscious turning away from all that is comprised in the term "the world." It is not fitting or seemly for a man of God to seek his recreation and pleasure only in wordly distractions and secular amusements, or to prefer the company of the laity to that of his fellow-priests. The priest who feels more at home and more sure of himself in fashionable salons and social lay circles than in the house of God exposes himself to the grave danger of losing the priestly spirit and of destroying the tender flower of a genuine priestly disposition that should bloom in his soul. He becomes a man

[13] Cf. Eph. 4: 23 f.
[14] See 1 Tim. 6: 11 f.

of the world and gradually ceases to be a true man of God.

The reserve which the Church at all times has recommended to its priests, both for their own good and for the good of their pastoral influence, has certainly not the purpose of making the priest a recluse from the world and from life; it surely does not imply that he must deny himself all social intercourse with the laity, or the aesthetic pleasures of culture and art. But this reserve does require that the priest, no matter in what surroundings or company he may find himself, always remember that he is a priest, a man consecrated to God; that he refrain from doing or saying anything at which the laity may legitimately take offense. To combine priestly tact and dignity on the one hand with a natural friendliness and an unforced courtesy on the other in perfect balance and harmony is an art which the man of God, living in the midst of the world, must master. It will preserve him both from any ungainly stiffness in his relations with men and also from any ill-timed insistence upon his dignity. Even in social circles the true man of God does not forget himself; no matter what his surroundings, he instinctively diffuses a definite spiritual atmosphere which has an edifying effect upon his environment, with the result that even in convivial company the boundaries of decorum and decency are never overstepped in the presence of the priest.

The spirit of a true man of God is necessary equipment for every priest on his ordination day. Thereafter, to foster its continued growth, he must practice a healthy asceticism. For a concrete example which will act as a check and a model in this most important work, let him rivet his eyes upon Christ; let him study the way this unique Man of

God acted among men, and His manner of consorting with others on social and friendly terms. Despite the majesty and dignity which never forsook Him, He was no eccentric among men, no solitary misanthrope. He took a friendly interest in the marriage feast at Cana, even working a miracle when the shortage of wine threatened the young couple with painful embarrassment. He stood in close friendship to Lazarus of Bethany and his two sisters. He mingled in a human and cordial manner with His disciples and Apostles. But with all His condescension and cordial relations toward men, He always remained dignified, always conscious of His Messianic vocation, never saying a word or making a gesture that would in the slightest degree offend against it. And so, in Christ we have the ideal *Homo Dei,* the one who presents the perfect example of inward disposition and outward deportment to every priest.

3. "PATTERN OF THE FLOCK"

Forma gregis ex animo. This New Testament designation of the priest is taken from the First Epistle of St. Peter. The Prince of the Apostles admonishes the heads of the various Christian communities in the following impressive manner: "Feed the flock of God which is among you, taking care of it, not by constraint, but willingly, according to God: not for filthy lucre's sake, but voluntarily: neither as lording it over the clergy, but being made a pattern of the flock from the heart." [15]

What St. Peter demanded of the elders in his day, the

[15] See I Pet. 5: 2 f.

infancy of Christianity, undoubtedly has equal force today, and will continue to apply as long as pastor and flock exist in the Church. No despotic power has been bequeathed to the heads of the Christian communities. They are never to rule by force. Rather, they should serve in love, standing before the congregation as models; they should lead the faithful, not only by words of instruction and admonition, but, what is far more important and necessary, by making their whole person and their entire way of life act as living patterns for the flock. The flock and each member of the flock should be able to look upon the shepherd as a model. As the shepherd is, so also should all members of the flock be.

The shepherd who, as priest and pastor of souls, is a leader and an inspiration to his congregation, has without question a sublime mission, a grave and responsible one, one that presupposes a humble but whole-hearted dedication to his vocation. Bearing that in mind, the Prince of the Apostles in his Epistle does not forget to call attention to the special heavenly reward that will come to those who faithfully discharge their office as heads of the community: "And when the prince of pastors shall appear, you [the heads] shall receive a never fading crown of glory." [16]

This obligation to lead blameless and model lives was also impressed by St. Paul upon his disciples Timothy and Titus, whom he had appointed to the episcopate. With urgency and warmth he admonished the former: "Be thou an example of the faithful in word, in conversation, in charity, in faith, in chastity." [17] No less emphatic are the

[16] *Ibid.*, 5: 4.
[17] See I Tim. 4: 12.

words he wrote to Titus, whom he had made head of the
Christian community in the island of Crete: "Young men,
in like manner, exhort that they be sober. In all things show
thyself an example of good works, in doctrine, in integrity,
in gravity." [18]

Pope St. Gregory the Great, in his immortal Pastoral Rule,
wrote a beautiful commentary on these exhortations of St.
Paul. He discusses at length the question about the qualifica-
tions and character of the one who is to take over the headship
of a Christian community; such a one must live and act as
head that he will be a pattern for the lives of others. "That
man, therefore, ought by all means to be drawn with cords
to be an example of good living who already lives spiritually,
dying to all passions of the flesh; who disregards worldly
prosperity; who is afraid of no adversity; who desires only
inward wealth; whose intention the body, in good accord
with it, thwarts not at all by its frailness, nor the spirit greatly
by its disdain: one who is not led to covet the things of
others, but gives freely of his own; who through the bowels
of compassion is quickly moved to pardon, yet is never bent
down from the fortress of rectitude by pardoning more than
is meet; who perpetrates no unlawful deeds, yet deplores
those perpetrated by others as though they were his own;
who out of affection of heart sympathizes with another's
infirmity, and so rejoices in the good of his neighbor as
though it were his own advantage; who so insinuates himself as an example to others in all he does that among them
he has nothing, at any rate of his own past deeds, to blush
for." [19]

[18] Tit. 2: 6 f.
[19] *Reg. Past.*, I, cap. 10 (*PL*, LXXVII, 23).

4. "GOOD SOLDIER OF JESUS CHRIST"

Bonus miles Jesu Christi. This title, which also belongs to a member of the New Testament priesthood, points in a different direction from the preceding ones. The very sound of it is military and warlike. The phrase comes down to us from St. Paul, who wrote to the Bishop of Ephesus, St. Timothy, as follows: "Labor as a good soldier of Christ Jesus. No man, being a soldier to God, entangleth himself with secular business; that he may please him to whom he hath engaged himself." [20] The content and form of this sentence remind us of the much older sentence in Holy Scripture to the effect that man's life on earth is after all a warfare; [21] St. Paul himself prefers to picture it as a battle which the Christian must wage.[22]

The priest, more than anyone else, must be a good soldier, a loyal warrior. In a far higher degree than the average Christian he has pledged himself to Christ, his general; at the time of his ordination he enlisted in the Lord's service and swore allegiance to His standard. His vocation and office compel him to fight for Christ and His kingship, to labor indefatigably for the maintenance and spread of Christ's Messianic realm, and to do so with his whole being, with the exertion of all his powers, with a singleness of purpose that makes him ignore all side issues. His military service in the army of Christ, both as a good soldier and as a captain of others, claims his entire person, his whole time, and all his energy.

[20] See II Tim. 2: 3 f.
[21] Job 7: 1.
[22] See I Tim. 1: 18.

When St. Paul calls the apostolic and the priestly office a military service and a warfare, he directs attention, as we have indicated, to yet another phase of the priesthood. Who is the enemy that threatens the kingdom and the rule of Christ? The kingdom of God on earth is menaced both from without and from within; the enemy from without attacks with the weapons of brute force and with the weapons of the spirit; the enemy from within makes use of heresies and schisms. It would be superfluous to count up in this place all the assaults that have been made upon the kingdom of Christ on earth in the course of the centuries, beginning with the days of our Lord Himself and continuing to most recent times. The Church has never been free of strife and persecution, never without martyrs who have shed their blood for her, never without loyal sons, both clerical and lay, who have heroically championed her rights.

The seminarian, hoping some day to dedicate himself to the service of Christ and the Church, must not lose sight of the fact that the lot of the kingdom of God, also in the present-day world, is one of battle and suffering, and that the Church can use only unselfish, self-sacrificing, and heroic soldiers in her priesthood. The candidate who remains cold and indifferent to the interests of Christ and of Christianity, who shrinks from hardship and battle, should never consider becoming a priest; he is not made of the stuff that is required for service on the firing line where the priest has his place. What intense and widespread opposition to Church and Christianity exists in the world of today! Deplorable and deep-rooted prejudice on the one hand, fanatical fury and diabolical hatred on the other, have again joined forces, over the entire world we might say, to make an assault against

God and His sovereignty. He whose intention it is to become a *bonus miles Jesu Christi* may not close his eyes to this fact, but must be able to summon up enough courage to face the issue unflinchingly. The future priest must remember that the kingdom of Christ on earth is not a triumphant but a militant Church, and that her battles must be waged principally by the clergy. Every priest, no matter where his field of labor, must join battle with sin, error, and unbelief, with delusion and seduction, and with all the satanic powers of hell.

In moving words and with similes taken from ancient methods of warfare, St. Paul describes the armor and equipment which every disciple of Christ, particularly every apostolic warrior, must wear and carry. Breastplate and helmet, shield and sword, are necessary to the soldier of Christ. "Therefore take unto you the armor of God, that you may be able to resist in the evil day, and to stand in all things perfect. Stand therefore, having your loins girt about with truth, and having on the breastplate of justice, and your feet shod with the preparation of the gospel of peace; in all things taking the shield of faith, wherewith you may be able to extinguish all the fiery darts of the most wicked one. And take unto you the helmet of salvation, and the sword of the Spirit (which is the word of God)." [23]

St. Paul amply demonstrated in his own life and person that the apostolic office was an unbroken series of hardships, sufferings, and battles. His brief autobiography,[24] sketched with a few bold strokes, makes fascinating reading, and we know that he is not boasting when at the end of his days he

[23] Eph. 6: 13–17; cf. I Thess. 5: 8.
[24] Cf. II Cor. 11: 23–33.

looks back upon his full life as an Apostle and makes the terse observation: "I have fought a good fight." [25]

As a good soldier and a brave warrior, the Apostle could feel himself one with his Lord and Master. Christ's primary purpose on earth was to announce the glad tidings and to complete the work of reconciling man with God. Nevertheless—and it seems almost like a paradox—He solemnly declared in the presence of His Apostles: "Do not think that I came to send peace upon earth: I came not to send peace, but the sword." [26] The sword, O Lord? The sword in your hand and in the hands of your priests? Yes, the Lord came to bring us the sword; not the bloody sword of earthly battle and mundane warfare (the Apostles were to return that sword to its scabbard),[27] but the sword of the spirit, the sword that cleaves mercilessly between truth and deception, between good and evil, between God and the world. This is the sword that the priest, as a good soldier of Christ, must carry and wield.

5. "MINISTER OF CHRIST AND DISPENSER OF THE MYSTERIES OF GOD"

Minister Christi et dispensator mysteriorum Dei. Another appropriate designation of the priest from St. Paul's pen. "Let a man so account of us as of the ministers of Christ, and the dispensers of the mysteries of God." [28]

This and nothing else is what St. Paul and his co-workers in the apostolate wished to be in the eyes of the community.

[25] See II Tim. 4: 7.
[26] Matt. 10: 34.
[27] *Ibid.*, 26: 52.
[28] See I Cor. 4: 1.

The expression shows that St. Paul was sublimely conscious of the dignity of the Apostolic office, and the outward esteem which for that reason he demands of the community is extraordinarily significant in a man who was so spiritual in his entire way of thought. But he did not demand too much for himself, for his co-workers, or for his successors.

The priest, like the Apostle, is a minister of Christ, a servant of his divine Lord and Master. The servant must do not his own will, but the will of him he serves. Christ Himself repeatedly stressed the fact that He had come to do not His own will, but the will of the Father who had sent Him.[29] He regarded it precisely as His life-work to fulfil faithfully the commandment of His Father.[30] Bowing to the will of his heavenly Father, He became obedient unto death, even to the death of the cross.[31]

Just as Christ was the minister of His heavenly Father, so the Apostles and their successors in office are the ministers of Christ, and are to be esteemed as such by the faithful. This consideration lights up another side of priestly vocation and, in contrast to the warlike aspect just spoken of, a more intrinsically vocational and functional side, which places the priest in the right relationship to Christ and the faithful. The new kingdom of God has only one Ruler and King, the divine Founder Himself, to whom all power is given in heaven and in earth.[32] As Son of God and Son of man, He gave the Church its constitution and its fundamental laws. The ecclesiastical hierarchy, that holy form of government

[29] John 4: 34; 5: 20; 6: 38.
[30] *Ibid.*, 14: 31.
[31] Phil. 2: 8.
[32] Matt. 28: 18.

which reaches its perfection in the papal monarchy, is His work. Not merely did He lay the foundation of this system; He continues to maintain it and to animate it with His Spirit. All the members of the hierarchy, from the highest who sits in the Chair of Peter to the humblest whose name is lost sight of, are but the representatives and the servants of their unseen Lord, who guides and rules the Church.

Above all, the simple priest, adorned with no hierarchical honors but, as an *alter Christus,* coming into immediate and personal contact with the faithful, should ever be filled with the holy and humble consciousness that he is a living tool in the hand of God, a chosen servant of Jesus Christ. In the first place, this consciousness reminds him of the sublime and elevating nature of his vocation; then, it preserves him from ruinous conceit and from the tragic danger of lording it over his flock or of regarding himself as the hub around which everything must turn; further, it reminds him of the truth that the flock committed to his care is not for his own benefit, but rather that he is their shepherd and that, as such, he must be the first servant of his flock.

As the minister of Christ, the priest is also the steward and dispenser of the mysteries of God. We have already considered the precious powers and treasures entrusted to the priest, which he is to administer and communicate to men —powers over the real and over the mystical body of Christ, treasures from the hand of God. They are mysteries of faith and grace, supernatural values all, that are placed in his hands. To him is delegated the announcing of the Gospel, the preaching of the faith and of the word of God. He it is, further, who supervises the graces of the sacraments and whose task consists in leading men to these treasures. "Here now it is required among the dispensers," writes St. Paul, "that a man be found faithful." [33]

Yes, all depends primarily upon the fidelity and conscientiousness with which the priestly steward discharges his office. But how does the faithful steward act? He does not think of himself, of his own honor or interests; he thinks only of the interests of the Master whose steward he is, and of the souls that have been entrusted to his care. Forgetful of self, shirking no exertion or hardship, he never neglects any duty which the conscientious exercise of his office imposes upon him. Such fidelity in service surely requires that he be permeated through and through with an ardent love of his neighbor, based on his love of God, and that at all times he feed the holy fire of apostolic zeal for souls in his priestly heart. If he is faithful in doing that, he needs no external canonical laws and no episcopal admonitions to keep him loyal to the unselfish fulfilment of his duties as steward, since the inner motive force, love of God and neighbor, is amply sufficient. And that is the way it should be. The real priest, especially one in the cure of souls, must draw his unfailing readiness and willingness to serve, his love and zeal for the administration of the divine mysteries, from an internal, supernatural conception of his vocation.

When that great shepherd of souls, St. Paul, set down the requirements demanded of a faithful steward, he could have appealed to his own example, to his countless sufferings and hardships in the service of the Gospel. As a matter of fact, he does exactly this in another place, and no one would think of charging him with untruthfulness or conceit because of

[33] See I Cor. 4: 2.

the self-assurance with which he speaks of himself and the administration of his office: "Giving no offence to any man, that our ministry be not blamed: but in all things let us exhibit ourselves as the ministers of God, in much patience, in tribulation, in necessities, in distresses, in stripes, in prison, in sedition, in labors, in watchings, in fastings, in chastity, in knowledge, in long-suffering, in sweetness, in the Holy Ghost, in charity unfeigned, in the word of truth, in the power of God; by the armor of justice on the right hand and on the left; by honor and dishonor, by evil report and good report; as deceivers, and yet true; as unknown, and yet known; as dying, and behold we live; as chastised, and not killed; as sorrowful, yet always rejoicing; as needy, yet enriching many; as having nothing, and possessing all things." [34]

6. "AMBASSADOR OF CHRIST"

Legatus Christi. Again, it is St. Paul who coined the phrase. "For Christ therefore we are ambassadors, God as it were exhorting by us." [35] In national political life, from which the Apostle obviously borrows this title, the ambassador, whose responsibility is to represent the interests of his country in the capital of a foreign power, exercises without question a gravely important office. A government, no matter what its political complexion, naturally expects that its envoy to a foreign nation not only will act outwardly in a manner befitting the dignity of the state he represents, but also that he will be fully competent to protect the national interests, and

[34] See II Cor. 6: 3–10.
[35] *Ibid.,* 5: 20.

finally that he will adhere strictly to the instructions he has received. An ambassador may not act according to his own personal preference or judgment; he must act in the spirit of the state he represents and in its name.

The idea of a sending had a prominent place in Jesus' conception of vocation. He often spoke of the fact that He had been sent into the world by His Father, and that His task consisted solely in fulfilling the Father's will. Just as He considers Himself the ambassador commissioned by His heavenly Father, so on the other hand He is fully conscious of His own regal dignity which gives Him the right to send out ambassadors of His own.

In this respect, the sending of the Twelve bears testimony to our Lord's awareness of His royal prerogative: "All power is given to me in heaven and in earth. Going therefore, teach ye all nations; baptizing them in the name of the Father, and of the Son, and of the Holy Ghost; teaching them to observe all things whatsoever I have commanded you: and behold I am with you all days, even to the consummation of the world." [36] And also the other sentence: "As the Father hath sent me, I also send you." [37] As He identifies Himself with the heavenly Father who had sent Him, so He identifies Himself with the Apostles whom He in turn sends: "He that heareth you, heareth me; and he that despiseth you, despiseth me; and he that despiseth me, despiseth him that sent me." [38] He assures them that their official acts will be ratified forthwith and will have validity in heaven: "Amen I say to you, whatsoever you shall bind upon earth, shall be bound

[36] Matt. 28: 18 f.
[37] John 20: 21.
[38] Luke 10: 16.

also in heaven; and whatsoever you shall loose upon earth, shall be loosed also in heaven." [39]

Such, in brief, are the most important instructions and mandates given by Christ, the Messias-King, to the Apostles at the time of their sending; with these He sent them out into the whole world as His representatives and ambassadors. Equipped with His divine authority and fulness of power, the Apostles and their successors in the teaching, sacerdotal, and pastoral office were to act in the name of Jesus.

An ambassador of Christ today is every priest sent into a parish by his bishop. Endowed with Christ's plenitude of power, he steps forth in the name of Christ to teach and exhort; when he celebrates mass and dispenses the sacraments, he acts in Christ's stead.

This thought of a sending, this consciousness that he has been commissioned by the highest authority, is something that has at all times given the Catholic priest a unique spiritual strength and also a profound sense of responsibility. Very accurately does Lippert in his discerning way write of the Catholic priest: "He knows and feels that the mission resting upon him is so great and so supremely important that his own person is completely covered and engrossed by it. . . . He no longer has any personal fitness of his own, and hence actually not even a right to existence independent of and separated from the purpose and authority of his mission." [40]

This strong, vigorous faith in his mission which in the last analysis goes back to God Himself can never desert the priest. This faith strengthens his vocational spirit, and is for the priest a valuable incentive to ascetic practice. It impels

[39] Matt. 18: 18; cf. John 20: 23.
[40] *Vom guten Menschen*, p. 234.

him to regulate his external behavior in a manner befitting the dignity of his vocation, and also to enter more and more into the spirit of Christ from whom he has received his consecration and sending. He should therefore never neglect the means that will make him grow in this spirit—prayer, meditation, and study.

The seminarian, who is to become a priest, must learn to use these same means early and to use them zealously, if he really desires to become an ambassador of Christ, not only in consecration and name, but also in spirit and essence. The process of growing and ripening in the spirit of Christ, the development of his soul according to the ideal of the Lord who will later send him forth, must be considered by the seminarian from the very beginning of his time of preparation as a holy duty that he may not put off; when the actual moment of ordination and sending arrives, he must long since have become imbued with the spirit of the divine Master and must be familiar with His thoughts.

7. "MEDIATOR OF GOD AND MEN"

Mediator Dei et hominum. This last title indicates that the priest, like his divine Model, is called upon to be a mediator between God and men. It is true that the New Testament Scriptures do not apply this title directly to Apostles and priests, but reserve it for Christ alone. However, with a legitimate broadening of the concept, the designation fits every Catholic priest.

With palpable emphasis St. Paul gives prominence to the office of Christ as mediator. "For there is one God, and one mediator of God and men, the man Christ Jesus: who gave himself a redemption for all." [41] St. Paul points out the singleness and the unique character of Christ's mediatorship. Just as there is only one God, one faith, one baptism,[42] so also there is only one mediator who has established the new covenant between God and men. In the Epistle to the Hebrews, Christ is described precisely in His character as mediator of the New Covenant.[43]

As there is no priesthood besides and outside the the eternal priesthood of Christ, so there is no mediatorship besides His and distinct from His. If in spite of this fact the Catholic priest is also called a mediator, he can be one only as an *alter Christus,* that is, in the continuation and operation of Christ's office as mediator.

This office of mediator is an exclusively priestly function. Viewed graphically, it simply means to stand between God and man, not separating them from each other, but uniting them. Protestantism misconceives the true essence of mediatorial activity when it denies every form of mediation and consequently every priesthood, on the mistaken assumption that such an office impedes the immediate union of the soul with God. The truth of the matter is that the priesthood acts not as a separating factor, but as a furthering and fructifying ligature between the soul and God.

Israel's priests also, especially the high priest, and the latter particularly in the impressively symbolic liturgy of the great Day of Atonement,[44] exercised essentially and by virtue of their vocation the office of mediator, preserving a living union between the people and Jahve. "Between the porch and the

[41] See I Tim. 2: 5 f.
[42] Eph. 4: 5.
[43] Cf. Heb. 8: 6; 9: 15; 12: 24.
[44] Cf. Lev. 16: 15 ff.

altar the priests the Lord's ministers shall weep, and shall say: Spare, O Lord, spare thy people: and give not thy inheritance to reproach, that the heathen should rule over them." [45]

This typical characteristic of Aaron's priesthood was not lacking in the New Testament, but rather found its fullest realization therein. By virtue of His dual nature as God-man, Christ was the born Mediator between God and mankind and, in visible and symbolic expression of His vocation as mediator, which He exercised in highest perfection at the time of His sacrificial death, He hung suspended between heaven and earth during that sacrifice.

All mediatorial activity exercised by the Catholic priesthood after Christ has its root and efficacy in our Lord and His sacrifice of atonement. By means of prayer and sacrifice the Catholic priest stands between God and the people. He, too, is to lift up his hands for the sins of men, sending up to God their plea for forgiveness. He approaches God as the representative of the people and returns to the people bringing God's blessing, grace, and help. He prays for sinners and for those who have gone astray; for those who struggle and fight; for those in danger and those who waver; for the good and the just; and lastly for the living and the dead. And he does all this not as a private person, but in the name of the Church and at her command. This eminently priestly duty finds solemn expression, for example, in the liturgy of Good Friday when the priest, as the servant of the Church, offers public suffrage for the various classes of mankind.

The words that Holy Writ places on the lips of the high priest Onias concerning the prophet Jeremias, whom the

[45] Joel 2: 17.

former saw in a vision, apply in still higher measure to the Catholic priest: "This is a lover of his brethren, and of the people of Israel: this is he that prayeth much for the people, and for all the holy city." [46]

[46] See II Mach. 15: 14.

CHAPTER V

The Priesthood and the Church

THE WORDS "priesthood and Church" need only be spoken to make us aware of the close relationship that has existed between the two from the very beginning to the present moment. They are not, however, identical. The priesthood is not the Church, nor is the Church the priesthood. In essence and extent the concept of Church goes far beyond that of priesthood, which is only a part of the vast ecclesiastical community. Nevertheless we must not forget that the priesthood, although it is only a part, and numerically only a small portion of the universal Church, is a part of more than ordinary significance, a part that, in a certain sense, comprises the most vital organs necessary for the life of the Church.

Many and far-reaching questions suggest themselves as soon as the relationship between Church and priesthood is subjected to closer scrutiny. For the sake of clarity we will group them under three main headings: 1. What significance has the priesthood for the Church? Or, to put it in another form, what does the priesthood accomplish for the Church? 2. What does the Church do for the priesthood? 3. What should be the personal attitude of the priest toward the Church?

I. WHAT DOES THE PRIESTHOOD ACCOMPLISH FOR THE CHURCH?

1. Since Christ, in the familiar metaphor, is described as
the head of His mystical body the Church, we may perhaps
extend the figure and speak of the priesthood as the heart
of this mystical body. If the heart is sound and the blood-
stream pure, the entire body is healthy. If the heart becomes weak or diseased so that this living motor no longer
forces sufficient fresh blood to the members of the body, the
whole man feels sick and miserable. Now, what is true of
the symbol is true also of what the symbol stands for,
namely, of the priesthood in its relation to the universal
Church. To drop the figure, there can be no question that
the inner life of the Church, as well as her outward growth,
is essentially dependent upon the priesthood. Schrörs' judgment is pertinent and accurate; he writes: "An old and
somber phrase, *omne malum a clero,* throws all blame for
ecclesiastical abuses upon the clergy. It was coined in melancholy times and had its historical justification. However, if
this lament, which many a high-minded person has uttered
with a sigh of resignation, is to receive the force of an
axiom, it must always be accompanied and completed by
the consoling companion phrase, *et omne bonum a clero.*
Only then is it incontestably true." [1]

The historian who employs this double axiom in study-
ing the development and activity of the Church in past
centuries will arrive at the conclusion that the growth and
flowering of the Church in the course of the ages, and also
her occasional periods of weakness and corruption, can in

[1] *Gedanken ueber zeitgemaesse Erziehung und Bildung der Geistlichen*
(1910), p. 1.

truth be ascribed to the prevailing condition of the clergy, both high and low. The real golden ages of the kingdom of God on earth—and we do not mean the periods when the external vesture of the Church sparkled in the radiance of great political power or in the brilliant light of cultural and artistic achievements, but rather those eras when the general religious and moral life of the faithful attained a very high level—those ages were, as a rule, also golden ages of the priesthood. They were periods when the essence of genuine priesthood was more profoundly and vividly understood, and when a rejuvenating power, reforming and renewing the sacerdotal state, went out from inspired leaders. To mention only a few, we point to such priestly leaders as St. Bernard of Clairvaux and St. Vincent de Paul, who brought about a new flowering of ecclesiastical life after periods of corruption and decline.

What is true of the past is true also of the present; nor can it be otherwise. As Schrörs says:

The priesthood occupies a central position in the Church. All that the Holy Spirit does not effect directly and mysteriously in the souls of men, all that is conditioned by external agencies and human co-operation, all the rich spiritual life in which eternal destinies are worked out, wells forth from that central font and flows back to it. Worship and sacrifice, sanctification through the sacraments, the preaching of the eternal verities, the instruction of youth and of the faithful at large, the government of parishes, the direction of ecclesiastical institutes, the cure of souls and the guidance of conscience in individual cases, everything that the Catholic expects of his Church in these respects, and all the confidence that he manifests toward her—all this is entrusted to the priesthood.[2]

[2] Op. cit., p. 1.

In very truth, the priesthood was instituted by Christ for the purpose of building up the Church both inwardly and outwardly. This building up of the Church as the mystical body of Christ was a favorite thought of St. Paul. With his keen discernment, he recognized this *aedificatio corporis Christi* as the true *opus ministerii* assigned to apostles, prophets, evangelists, pastors, and doctors.[3] The faithful as a whole appeared to the Apostle as a massive and majestic temple in the course of construction, a temple resting on the foundation of the Apostles and prophets, with Christ as the cornerstone.[4] Foundation and cornerstone have been laid; now, according to St. Paul, the work of completing the structure must go on until it has become "a temple, holy to the Lord."[5]

The priesthood has the task of continuing the work begun by the Apostles and prophets, the task of finding new stones for this living temple and of incorporating them in the structure. The priest is the one who assembles these new stones, that is, the one who adds to the number of the faithful; he is also the one who smooths the stones at hand, that is, the one who sedulously watches over and sanctifies those already in the ranks of the faithful. For to him are entrusted the word of God and the treasures of grace. In this sense we may say, preserving the metaphor of St. Paul, that the priesthood as a whole and each individual priest are in truth temple-builders, chosen and authorized by God; they are to perform their task according to the specifications and purposes of God, and also with

[3] Cf. Eph. 4: 12.
[4] Cf. *ibid.*, 2: 20 f.
[5] *Ibid.*, 2: 21.

His grace and power. Such is their mission in regard to the vast structure of the visible Church as a whole and also in regard to the invisible sanctuary of the Lord in the individual soul.

A brief glance at the ecclesiastical life of the present, with its widespread ramifications, its prodigious tasks and difficulties, is sufficient to make us realize the altogether indispensable character of priestly activity. The Church of our day would never be able to fulfil her spiritual and moral obligations if a trained and zealous clergy were not at her command. The pastoral ministry in town and country is growing more complex with each passing year, as the economic needs of the people increase; the menace to faith and morals from socialism, communism, and an excessive nationalism is daily becoming more ominous; the hostility of a militant atheism to all things Christian is mounting steadily. These grave problems must be met and solved by the clergy, and specifically by the clergy engaged in the care of souls. At intervals, popes and bishops, viewing the world from their points of vantage, issue clarifying and directive instructions that shine like beacons into the darkness and murk of deception and error. But, as a rule, the lower clergy have the grave responsibility of carrying these messages to the common people in such a way that they will have the greatest possible effect and produce practical good.

The Church, of course, considers the co-operation of the laity indispensable, today perhaps more than ever before, in view of the more pressing demands made upon her, particularly in the fields of charity and pastoral guidance. She gladly welcomes all the assistance offered her by the apos-

tolate of the laity and the various charitable organizations
for the care of youth, and the like. But lay aid can never
take the place of priestly activity. Even prescinding from
the fact that the sacrifice of the mass and the administration
of the sacraments are committed exclusively to the consecrated hands of the priest, the guidance and inspiration
that only a priest can give will always be required even in
those fields where the co-operation of the laity is most desirable and necessary.

What has been said of the grave responsibilities confronting the Church in the fields of charity and pastoral guidance is equally true of the scientific and cultural tasks of
the Church, and of the serious economic, social, and political
questions which she must face. Whenever these matters,
which are partly of a non-ecclesiastical nature, affect the
interests of the Church—and that is almost always the case—
the Church has the duty to insist that the principles and
dictates of the Gospel be given proper recognition also in
these fields. When such a question arises, she welcomes with
joy and gratitude the aid of Catholic lay champions, without at the same time desiring to dispense with the powerful
support given by the priesthood. Priests are always among
the first who act as the mouthpiece of the teaching and
ruling Church. Through them she makes known her mind
and asserts her rights in meeting and solving even those
problems that lie along the borderline of her province.

The Church owes a specific and more than ordinary debt
of gratitude to those members of her priesthood who have
done pioneer and advanced work in the domain of ecclesiastical science. Almost all the outstanding names in philosophy, theology, and allied sciences, have been those of

bishops and priests. Lay authorities, such as, for example, Tertullian in the early Church, have been relatively few in number. Among the clergy who have distinguished themselves in this field we find stars of the first magnitude, men of brilliant intellect who devoted their splendid talents to theological research and to the scientific justification and systematization of revealed truths. Where would Christian philosophy and theology be without the immortal contributions of a St. Augustine or a St. Thomas Aquinas, to say nothing of other shining but lesser lights? Practically always the the defense of revealed truth against the intellectual attacks launched by the Church's enemies has been entrusted to the hands of priestly scholars and theologians. In almost every instance they have been the ones who met, with scientific weapons, the assaults of the enemies of the faith and, in hard-fought battles, carried off the palm of victory for the glory of the Church—the secular and the regular clergy vying with each other in noble rivalry. The Church no doubt is deeply indebted to many scholarly laymen who, in their own specialties, have lent their fine talents to the defense of divine revelation. But the contributions of the lay faithful in the matter of guarding and expounding the deposit of faith are far surpassed by the accomplishments of the clergy, especially in the technical fields of Catholic philosophy and theology.

In the interest of fairness and truth, however, we must also admit that the ranks of the clergy have supplied, in the form of heretics and schismatics, the most dangerous and destructive enemies that the Church has had to contend with. The most disastrous heretical movements which have shaken the universal Church, namely, Arianism and Lutheranism, are coupled with the names of apostate Catholic priests. *Omne malum a clero.* On the other hand, the staunchest champions of orthodoxy have also come from the midst of the clergy.

2. As to the activity of the Church in the mission field, we again find that the priesthood has always occupied the dominant position in the work of spreading the kingdom of God among the heathen peoples of the world. From St. Paul to St. Boniface, St. Patrick, St. Francis Xavier, and the rest, all the great missioners of the Church have been members of the clergy. Notwithstanding the fact that devoted lay brothers and nuns outnumber priests in the mission field, it cannot be denied that the actual direction of the foreign missions of the Church, today as heretofore, rests with the priesthood, specifically with the regular clergy.

The anointed missionary priest who journeys to pagan lands is and remains the soul of all missionary endeavor and labor. He has received his commission and his spiritual power from the Church, and he preaches the Gospel in her name. He is and must be the one whose heart burns with undying love for Christ, the one whose missionary zeal and ardent interest in the conversion of pagan peoples may never slacken, without endangering the whole of missionary activity. The missionary spirit must burn so brightly in his priestly soul that he will be able to inspire his co-workers, and fan into flame a zeal that has perhaps waned because of the many difficulties encountered. At all times, if not always in the same number, the Church has produced magnanimous priestly volunteers ready to leave home and country and to brave hardships and privations, even a martyr's death, in order to carry the light of the Gospel to those who still dwell in the darkness of paganism. Very often such priests have been called upon to make the supreme sacrifice, and the soil of the mission field is reddened with their blood. We can say with truth that the history of Catholic missionary activity is a glorious page not only in the annals of the Church as a whole, but also and particularly in the story of the priesthood.

If we now sum up in a retrospective glance what the clergy at home and in the field afar has accomplished and continues to accomplish for the Church, we must admit that the total is enormous and of extraordinary value. Nor is the Church alone convinced of this fact. The sworn enemies of the Church and of Christianity recognize it just as clearly and make their first assault upon the priesthood, whenever they plan an attack upon the Church. There can be no doubt about it; in the eyes of her enemies, the priesthood of the Catholic Church is always regarded, and rightly so, as her first line of defense, as the strong phalanx which they feel they must overcome at the very start of any campaign against her.

2. WHAT DOES THE CHURCH DO FOR THE PRIESTHOOD?

In this section we purpose to answer briefly the second question that we have proposed for consideration. Speaking in a general way, we may assert that, while the priesthood has accomplished much for the Church, the Church in turn has done much for the priesthood. The education and training of her priests, as also their growth in the way of holiness, have from the beginning been near to the heart of the Church; popes and bishops, as well as the Catholic laity, have taken an active part therein.

With motherly solicitude the Church accompanies the candidate along the stages that lead him to the priesthood, from the first sprouting of the seed of vocation to the imposition of hands by the bishop. She gravely admonishes those in the pastoral ministry, especially pastors, to pay special attention to the souls of young men who give evidence of the first signs of vocation; they should carefully and protectingly nurture the tender seed of vocation planted in such souls by almighty God.[6]

1. From earliest days the Church has kept a watchful eye upon the systematic education of priestly recruits, always with the intention of accepting only worthy and fit candidates into the sacerdotal state. With this end in view, she has created special institutions and schools, which trace their origin back to the first Christian centuries.[7] Over and above its interest in the moral regeneration of the existing clergy, the Council of Trent was chiefly concerned about the recruiting and training of a suitable sacerdotal increase. The well-known decree of the Council regarding the establishment of seminaries directed that a separate institution for the training of candidates for the priesthood be established in every diocese.[8] This decree brought order and method into the education of young clerics; and the Church, in the face of many difficulties, gradually succeeded in introducing the so-called Tridentine seminaries into almost all countries.

A quasi-exception exists today in those dioceses of Germany and Austria where candidates for the priesthood take

[6] Cf. CIC, can. 1353.

[7] Cf. Siebengartner, *Schriften und Einrichtungen zur Bildung der Geistlichen* (1902), pp. 6 ff.

[8] Sess. XXIII, cap. 18. Cf. also Siebengartner, *op. cit.*, pp. 85 ff.

their scholastic courses at the university; in these circumstances, the moral and ascetic training of the candidates is provided for by separate episcopal foundations, where the students live during their time of preparation. Another exceptional situation is found in the Catholic universities recently established, especially in France; such institutions have faculties of theology, which equip candidates for the priesthood with their technical knowledge. But in these cases also, as has been the practice in Rome for centuries, the Tridentine influence is evident in the establishment of special colleges, which stand next to and separate from the university and serve the same moral and spiritual purposes as the episcopal foundations in Germany and Austria. Recently, and for the first time with universal application, the Church has made seminary training or its equivalent compulsory during the entire duration of philosophical and theological study.[9] Exceptions, however, are permitted at the discretion and responsibility of the individual bishops.[10]

Moreover, in the last few centuries, and especially in the last decades, the Church has given increased attention to the specifically technical training of priestly candidates.[11] The program set down by the popes themselves never varies; it calls for more thorough and more timely training of seminarians, a training that takes into consideration changing conditions and that meets the requirements of a new age. The highest ecclesiastical authority gladly permitted and encouraged a free expression of opinion by competent educators on this vitally important program, with the result

---

[9] CIC, can. 972, 1354, § 1, 2.
[10] *Ibid.*, can. 972, § 1.
[11] Cf. Schrörs, *op. cit.*, pp. 6 ff.

that an imposing literature on the subject came into existence, especially in France and Italy. The pertinent stipulations contained in the New Code of Canon Law and providing, in a general way, for a two-year course in philosophy and a four-year course in theology[12] may be regarded as the crystallized product of this free airing of views, which had a fundamental influence upon the policy of the Church in the matter of training clerics. From the immediate past we have the significant constitution of Pius XI, *Deus scientiarum,* issued on June 12, 1931; its purpose was to raise the study of theology to a still higher and more scientific level.[13]

Not only the Roman pontiffs of earlier and of more recent times, but also the individual bishops of the different countries have conspicuously manifested to the world their great pastoral concern and love for the clergy. Episcopal and synodal decrees dealing in detail with the moral sanctification of the clergy, the improvement of their spiritual way of life, and the training of priestly recruits, are without number. Probably no provincial or diocesan synod in the centuries after Trent has neglected to treat these topics at length.[14]

If we take a general view of the entire subject with the purpose of summarizing the essential ideas and viewpoints expressed in these efforts of the Church to regulate the training of clerics, we must admit that the Church, in her motherly solicitude, has set up very high requirements for her priests and for priestly candidates. These requirements far exceed the standard of education and training recognized

[12] CIC, can. 1365, § 1, 2.
[13] *Acta Apost. Sed.,* XXIII (1931), pp. 241–80.
[14] Cf. Siebengartner, *op. cit.,* pp. 98 ff.

for other states in life that have a similar social status. They demand not only an intellectual and moral fitness, but also bodily integrity, physical and mental health, and good family background. As a rule, only the best sons of the people are accepted into the priesthood by the Church. Ecclesiastical impediments based on defects bar from holy orders a whole series of persons, whether these defects are present with or without moral guilt. Viewed objectively and with the good of the whole in mind, this apparent severity, which is at times bitterly resented by those personally affected, is simply another proof of the tender solicitude of the Church for the welfare and good repute of a state that holds first place in her affections.

2. And another thing must not be forgotten. The Church prays for her priests; the teaching and the believing Church, the supreme shepherd and the faithful flock, implore God's blessing upon the priesthood. Particularly on the ember days (the ordination days of old) the Church urges all the faithful to beseech heaven for the divine gift of good priests; in her liturgy on those days she herself prays fervently to God for the same intention. It is a pity that this significance of the ember days has largely disappeared from the religious consciousness of our people in recent times, due no doubt to the circumstance that the conferring of holy orders is no longer confined exclusively to those days. The Church prays for the awakening and preservation of vocations to the priesthood, prays in her liturgy for the priests themselves, prays for the steadfastness and perseverance of her clergy.

The sublime ritual with which the Church leads the new Levites step by step through the minor and major orders and into her sanctuary overflows with prayers, supplications, and blessings. To see and hear how she uses the lips of the consecrating bishop to beg God and all the saints of heaven for grace and blessing upon the group of prostrate candidates is profoundly moving. Two things stand out clearly in the rite of ordination, especially to priesthood: a holy earnestness testifying to the sense of grave responsibility with which the Church performs the imposition of hands, and also the motherly kindness and love with which, as it were, she embraces the newly ordained. They are her "dearly beloved children," *filii dilectissimi*, to whom, after conferring the order of priesthood, she directs her last admonitions, recommending them to the protection of God's mercy.[15]

In truth, the Church embraces her priestly workers with the love of a father and a mother; her parental solicitude accompanies them through life, and it is with an almost boundless confidence that she entrusts her most sacred possessions and treasures to them.

3. The Church has also shown her great concern and love for the priesthood in other ways.[16] In the course of the ages she has bestowed on clerics a number of privileges that give them precedence over the laity. These include personal inviolability, the right to a special court, immunity from certain services and burdens, the assurance of a proper maintenance, and various privileges of an honorary nature. We will treat briefly the most important of these clerical privileges recognized by canon law.

First of all, the Church desires her priests to be protected

---

[15] Cf. *Pontificale Romanum, de ordine presbyteri.*
[16] Cf. Koeniger, *Katholisches Kirchenrecht* (1926), pp. 154 ff., 373, 376.

in public from personal violence; hence she burdens such offenses with the grave nature of a sacrilege and punishes them with penalties that take effect *ipso facto*. The seriousness of the offense is determined by the rank of the offended person (*privilegium canonis*).[17] Wherever possible, she has always taken care to provide that the official priestly duties, especially the celebration of mass, be performed under the protection of the civil authority.

In accordance with a desire of the Church that goes back to most ancient times but that is only partially realized today, clerics are not to appear in the civil forum; all litigation, whether among themselves or with the laity, is to be settled in the ecclesiastical court (*privilegium fori*).[18] In this matter also the Church is guided solely by the motive of protecting, in the interests of religion and of the sacerdotal state, the good repute and honor of clerics, who would all too easily be laid open to bitter attacks and painful exposures in civil trials. It is deplorable that the recognition of this legitimate privilege is thwarted by almost insuperable difficulties in modern states.

Further, the Church desires her priests to possess a form of immunity that relieves them of military duty and of other public services incompatible with the nature and dignity of the sacerdotal state (*privilegium immunitatis*).[19] It is not her fault that many modern nations do not recognize this exemption, especially in regard to military service and the bearing of arms. Some states, however, have shown a

[17] Cf. CIC, can. 119, 2343.
[18] *Ibid.*, can. 120, § 1.
[19] *Ibid.*, can. 121, 139. See also Koeniger, *op. cit.*, p. 156.

laudable understanding of the Church's position. During the World War, Germany refrained from calling to the colors any clerics in major orders, even in those critical stages of the struggle when the need for man power was most acute.

Mention must also be made of the privilege whereby the Church strives to insure clerics of an income sufficient for a suitable livelihood, even when judgments against their property have been obtained (*privilegium competentiae*).[20] Today, the recognition and scope of this privilege are, of course, dependent upon state law.

In addition to these privileges, granted for the protection of the priestly calling, the Church has won for the clergy a series of honorary privileges, the sole purpose of which is to raise this state in public estimation. In a general way, she demands that the laity show deference to the priest and respect for the dignity of his office.[21] Further, she accords the clergy the right of precedence (*praecedentia*).[22] Then, the clergy are entitled to a special place in church (in the presbyterium or chancel), and they have a claim to certain titles of honor (your reverence, etc.). Distinctive dress is also an honorary privilege of the clerical state, and the Church has always taken pains to obtain in various countries legal protection for the wearing of clerical garb.

4. Lastly, the Church is concerned about a sufficient income and a suitable livelihood for those who serve her as clerics and priests. According to general canon law, priest-

[20] CIC, can. 122.
[21] *Ibid.*, can. 119.
[22] *Ibid.*, can. 106.

hood may be conferred only under a definite title which guarantees the one ordained a fitting maintenance for his entire life. The whole development of the system of ecclesiastical benefices, which often involved popes and bishops in sharp conflicts with the civil power, is intimately connected with this solicitude of the Church for her clergy. She has always striven to couple a corresponding income (*beneficium*) with every permanent ecclesiastical office (*officium*). On the one hand, she forbids the priest to live beyond his station and in a luxurious manner, and obligates him to devote to pious causes the superfluities accruing to him from churchly sources; on the other hand, she does not wish her priests to be permanently exposed to poverty and need. In prudent appraisal of actual conditions, the Church rightly considers these extremes incompatible with the priestly state, and her desire is to shield the individual priest both from superfluous wealth and from grinding poverty.

Summing up, we may say that the Church demands much of those who dedicate their lives to her service, much in the way of moral and physical fitness, much in the way of spiritual preparation and scientific training, much in the way of personal consecration and fidelity to the duties of their vocation; but at the same time she manifests a most anxious concern for the spiritual and material welfare of her servants. On this score, too, she has a perfect right to the ancient and beautiful title, *pia mater Ecclesia.* The popular adage, "To live under the crozier is to lead a pleasant life," may be more or less invidious, but the words can be understood in a good sense, and every priest who is a faithful servant of the Church has found them fully confirmed.

3. WHAT SHOULD BE THE PERSONAL ATTITUDE OF THE PRIEST TOWARD THE CHURCH?

We do not intend, in this place, to speak of everything that the true priest and the divinely called candidate to the priesthood owe to the Church. Our purpose is simply to point out more accurately the fundamental personal and mental attitude that should be theirs. Love for love, loyalty for loyalty. These words sum up everything that is essential, and indicate the threefold duty that the priest has toward the Church, namely, to think and feel with the Church, to behave with reverence and tact wherever the Church is concerned, and to love the Church with unswerving devotion.

1. We designedly put in first place the duty of thinking with the Church. The priest must be a man of the Church; as such, he must stand with both feet and without wavering on the principles of the Church. In any situation that may some time or other confront him, the genuine priest is always found on the side of the Church. Not only is he outwardly loyal to the Church; he thinks and feels with her; the so-called *sentire cum Ecclesia* has gone over into his flesh and blood, and determines the trend of his whole life. In good and in evil days his complete attachment to the Church resembles the purest conjugal love; he rejoices with the Church whenever the occasion presents itself; he sorrows with her when she is afflicted with sufferings. For better or for worse he is bound to the Church; her lot is his lot; the Church is all and everything to him.

The man of the Church has his finger on the pulse of the Church's life; he senses the slightest movements, the most delicate throbbings, the most intimate yearnings that pulsate through the mystical body of Christ. He has an instinctive perception for what is ecclesiastical and what is not, even when no express command or prohibition exists; he has a heart for the Church, a heart that beats for the Church, a heart that is large enough to embrace the sublime tasks of the kingdom of God on earth.

To grow more and more in this spirit and disposition must be the uninterrupted striving of every priestly candidate and every priest. If this spirit is carefully nurtured, another and baneful spirit, peculiar to the youth of our day, will never arise at all or will be speedily suppressed. We refer to the evil spirit of carping criticism and malicious faultfinding. This is the deadly poison that can infect and kill a priestly vocation. If this spirit is not kept under rigid control, the seminarian or the priest exposes himself to the danger of losing all interior peace of soul. Particularly in a seminarian, this ill-natured and continuous faultfinding, this mental quirk that makes him feel compelled to pass adverse criticism upon all practices and regulations of the Church, is like a wedge driven into his inmost soul and splitting his whole personality in two. On such a broken foundation priestly vocation and priestly ideals cannot long endure; they totter and slowly crumble to the ground.

It is an elementary requirement of his vocation that the seminarian strive from the very beginning of his course to acquire the proper attitude toward the Church. Does this perhaps mean that he should stand before the Church like a blind man, that he should follow her passage through history with unseeing eyes? Or should he be made to believe that there has been nothing imperfect or blameworthy in the externals of the Church of yesterday or today, that the outward vesture of the Church is altogether without spot or blemish? The answer to these questions is an emphatic "no." The Church, as a visible phenomenon composed of imperfect men, has a considerable share of the imperfections and weaknesses found in everything earthly and human. In her long course through the changing centuries, her outward garb has occasionally been torn and stained. Who would wish to deny it? But the outward form of the Church is only one, and indeed the human, side of the bride of Christ. This heavenly spouse has another, a supernatural and divine side, and that is the Church as the Lord fashioned her, without wrinkle or spot or any other defect, a Church holy and spotless.[23]

A loyal son of the Church, be he seminarian or priest, is familiar with this double aspect of the Church of Christ; he knows that defects and abuses affect only the external side of the Church, leaving her real nature unimpaired. He recognizes these weaknesses and faults, he sees them clearly and with unblinking eyes; he does not condone, but condemns them. However, this pained recognition of an evil has nothing in common with a spirit of carping criticism or of pharisaical self-righteousness; it springs from his love for the Church, which is like the love of a child for its mother. "Charity," writes St. Paul, "beareth all things . . . , endureth all things." [24] An open eye and clear-sighted vision, accompanied by reverence and love, characterize the attitude that should be taken by the seminarian and the priest toward the faults and weaknesses of the external Church.

[23] Eph. 5: 27.
[24] See I Cor. 13: 7

2. Something else belongs in this place, something that flows spontaneously from love and reverence and makes the loyal cleric always temperate and reserved in his criticisms of the Church: a feeling of delicacy and tact. A well-mannered son does not readily speak of the shortcomings and moral lapses of his own father, even though fully aware of them. Filial piety seals his lips and prompts him to bear his sorrow in silence. When he does speak of his distress, he does so only to relieve his afflicted heart, and still more to seek confidential advice regarding ways and means to remedy the sad condition. Even then the tactful son avoids any expression that could give pain or offense.

The relation of a priest or seminarian to the Church is that of a child to its father and mother. An innate sense of delicacy preserves him at all times from a spirit of self-righteousness and prevents him from sitting in judgment upon the Church, Church ordinances, or ecclesiastical abuses, and from speaking about them in public, especially in the presence of the laity. This tact, born of filial reverence and gratitude, tells him that precisely in such circumstances a discreet silence is far more becoming than insolent and adverse criticism. The wounds and defects that mar the body of the Church are visible to him, and they fill his soul with sadness, but they do not lessen his love for the Church. On the contrary, they spur him on to greater love; they fill him with the ardent desire to do whatever he can to help the Church in her tribulations and necessities. Nor should the seminarian's enthusiasm for his vocation suffer at the sight of such imperfections and abuses in the Church, no matter how shocking they may be; rather they should purify it, and impel him to dedicate himself more unreservedly to the service of the Church.

But one dangerous snare that the seminarian must scrupulously avoid is the temptation to make a senseless and unfortunate distinction between an ideal Church and the Church of reality. No such thing as a dual Church exists; there is only one Church, and that is the Church as she is in reality. This concrete Church, of course, has the duty and also the inner urge to approximate, in her internal and external development, more and more the highest ideal. Hence it is futile, even impossible, to approve an ideal Church removed from reality, and to condemn the Church that actually exists. Experience proves that the danger in such conceptions and distinctions, which in the last analysis spring perhaps from an unconscious but unhealthy subjectivism, lies principally in this, that they soon lead in practice to a hostile attitude toward the existing Church, and in the end to complete apostasy. This lamentable consequence in itself should prompt every Catholic, and in particular every seminarian, to suppress from the very start any tendency to make such distinctions and to avoid, as a matter of principle, all such purposeless subtleties. The divine-human institution as it exists in reality is the only one that must be recognized as the true Church of Christ; to it belong our reverence, our obedience, our love, and our loyalty.

3. The last words of the preceding paragraph are profoundly significant and define the attitude of seminarian and priest to the Church. St. Paul assures us that Christ, the Founder of the Church, loves her and has delivered Himself up for her. The Apostle holds up this steadfast love of

Christ for the Church, a love that He sealed with His death, as a model for the conjugal love and fidelity that should characterize husband and wife [25] Where the Church is concerned, a reverential love and a loyal devotion that can be diverted by nothing, neither by mockery, nor scorn, nor calumny, least of all by unjust persecution, must fill the heart of every true Catholic, and certainly of every seminarian and priest. Faithlessness and treachery to the Church are the greatest dishonor that a Catholic, and *a fortiori* a Catholic priest, can load upon himself.

The loyalty with which the seminarian and the priest cling to the Church manifests itself outwardly in glad submission to ecclesiastical authority and in complete obedience to the Church's pronouncements and laws, whether they are definitions of faith or disciplinary decrees. For loyal sons of the Church, the ancient axiom is decisive: *Roma locuta est, causa finita est.*

[25] Cf. Eph. 5: 25 f.

CHAPTER VI

The Priesthood and the People

I. THE SOCIAL CHARACTER OF THE PRIESTHOOD

1. Our Lord truly said that His Apostles and disciples were not of this world. Nor may the priesthood be of this world. Nevertheless, Christ sent His Apostles out into the world, to all nations and peoples—a clear indication that the Apostles and their successors in office were not to lead an isolated life, far from the haunts of men; rather, they were to seek out men, their place was to be in the midst of human society. In this way did Christ Himself reveal the social character of the apostolate and of the priesthood; the priest, as well as the Apostle, exists not for himself, but for mankind.

This thought expresses a fundamental characteristic of the secular priesthood. No one may or should become a priest for his own sake, whether the motive be that of personal piety or of personal salvation. On the contrary, the person who intends to embrace this vocation must be convinced that he is becoming a priest for the community, for his fellow-men, for the care and salvation of the souls of others.

The basic program for every secular priest is outlined in

the words of the Epistle to the Hebrew: *Ex hominibus assumptus pro hominibus constituitur.*[1] Divine vocation takes the young man destined for the priesthood from the midst of the people, transforms and ennobles him, and then gives him back to the people. This is the manner in which the priesthood of the New Testament renews and rejuvenates itself. Unlike the priesthood of Israel, which was joined to a definite tribe and was handed down by carnal generation as an inheritance from father to son, the priesthood of Jesus Christ uses the entire Catholic faithful as the fruitful soil from which it brings forth a never failing harvest of new priestly incumbents. Precisely this method of obtaining fresh recruits for the sacerdotal state reveals the natural and close relationship that exists between priest and people.

Christ Himself was certainly not of this world. Yesterday, today, and forever, the eternal Son of the heavenly Father belongs to a totally different world, the supernatural and divine world of God. Yet He came into this world. As God-man, He was born into the race of men, assuming the flesh and blood of a human nature that would enable Him to redeem men and win them for heaven.

In the last analysis, what was the compelling motive that brought the eternal Son of God down from heaven? The answer can be given in one word: love. Loving men and their immortal souls with all the ardor of His Sacred Heart, He walked on earth as mankind's best and truest friend. Notwithstanding His preference for seclusion and solitude, He was no hermit holding Himself aloof from the world of men; rather, He associated freely with His people,

[1] Heb. 5: 1.

He considered Himself one of the human community in which He lived.

Nor was the situation any different in the case of St. Paul, that great pastor of the infant Church. Immediately following his conversion, he spent some time in the solitude of the desert in order to complete the transformation that had taken place in his soul, but the apostolic urge soon drove him back to the world of men. In the plan of God he had become the vessel of election, to carry the name of the Lord before Gentiles and kings and the children of Israel.[2] For that reason and with indefatigable zeal, he turned his steps toward the most populous cities of the ancient world. He hastened to Antioch and Ephesus, to Corinth and Athens, and finally to Rome. Thus the great cities became the first centers of Christianity, while the old pagan religion continued to live on in the country districts.

We call attention at this point to the beginnings of Christianity simply to show how the strong tendency to labor among the people and to act as shepherd to the souls of men was characteristic of the apostolic office from the very beginning. And how could it be otherwise? The Lord's express command to preach the Gospel to every creature forbade the withdrawal of the Apostles and their fellow-workers from the world; it literally compelled them to place themselves wholly at the service of mankind. That was the purpose for which they had become Apostles, that was the reason why the Lord had selected them and sent them forth.

The mission of the Apostles sheds the clearest possible light upon the reason for the priesthood's existence among

[2] Acts 9: 15.

men. The pre-eminently social character of this vocation, the reason why it must, so to speak, keep its face turned toward the world, is best indicated by the term "the pastoral ministry" and all that it implies. We use the phrase here, not in the somewhat restricted sense that it has today and that contrasts the priest in the cure of souls with all other priests, but in a broader sense as meaning any and all activities for the welfare of his fellow-man, in which the priest as priest is engaged.

2. Understood in this sense, the priest in the pastoral ministry is contrasted with the hermit and the monk of past and present times. Their ways go in different directions. The monk who abandons the world and desires to serve God within the confines of a monastery, or the hermit who flees from the haunts of men and leads a solitary life in his little cell, is concerned exclusively with the sanctification and salvation of his own soul, without thinking, at least directly and primarily, of the salvation of others. Pastoral activity in the proper sense has always been foreign to monasticism, even though occasionally and by way of exception outstanding missioners and shepherds of souls have come forth from the solitude of the cloister. St. Boniface, who was a monk of the Benedictine Order, is a case in point. Moreover, everyone is familiar with the extraordinary contributions that classical monasticism, which today lives on among the Benedictines and in the religious orders related to them, has made and continues to make to the cause of the ministry in various countries. But the fact remains that this pastoral activity took place more under the compulsion of special conditions than from any internal urge or calling.

The situation is different, of course, with regard to the religious orders and congregations that came into existence later with the avowed purpose of pursuing pastoral aims; they regard apostolic activity as their primary duty. But in their case the idea of monasticism, as such, is abandoned, and the pastoral idea has been moved into the foreground. The members of these apostolic orders and communities, therefore, rightly think of themselves more as shepherds of souls than as monks living for themselves.

But these exceptions do not militate against the fact that the one who by virtue of his vocation exercises the pastoral ministry is not the religious, but the so-called secular priest. His proper field of labor is the cure of souls in all its manifold branches; he is the regular and ordinary shepherd of the people, while the order priest assists in this apostolic work only on certain extraordinary occasions, such as at the time of a mission or a retreat.

It is altogether true that the secular priest may not be of this world, even though he must live in the midst of the world. His place is among men and for men; not flight from the world in the monastic or eremitical sense, but love for the world and for men after the manner and example of Christ, constitutes the charisma of the priesthood. Without the least doubt, as we have repeatedly said before, the secular priest also has the grave obligation of personal sanctification; but in contrast to the monk and the hermit, this striving after sanctity is not the beginning and end of his vocation. The essential task which his priestly office imposes upon him consists rather in the sanctification and salvation of the souls of his fellow-men.

Therefore it would be a fundamental misconception and

distortion of the aim of priestly vocation if a person were to enter the priesthood from the motive of personal sanctification. Such a one would only be deceiving himself and would inevitably lay himself open to dangerous disillusionment. Where this motive is paramount, that is, where an extraordinary degree of personal holiness is looked upon as the primary goal, the decision of the candidate should be in favor of one of the many religious orders whose professed purpose is to lead their members along the road of the evangelical counsels to the greatest possible height of personal perfection. The secular priesthood, on the other hand, must always consider the sanctification of others as its first and most important duty.

The seminarian should have a clear understanding of this difference between the secular priesthood and the religious state, especially when he is undecided, and hesitates between the two. As a rule, the first thing he notices is what the two states have in common, namely, that the members of both are priests. But he must also consider the essential differences that exist between the religious state (the missionary congregations of later date included) on the one hand, and the secular priesthood with its express vocation to save souls, on the other. Many are suited for the one vocation, not for the other. The personal disposition and the spiritual inclination of the candidate play a most important part in the final decision.

2. THE PRIEST AS THE SHEPHERD OF SOULS

1. When we read in the Epistle to the Hebrews that "every high priest taken from among men, is ordained for

men," [3] the duties thus outlined must obviously be limited to a definite sphere. The question is: What aspect of the welfare of mankind requires the labor and assistance of the priest? The individual, as well as the human race in general, has a multiplicity of needs requiring the attention and ministrations of others—physical and health needs, educational and cultural needs, needs of an economic, a social, and a political nature. The province reserved to specifically priestly service lies beyond the sphere of the interests and wants just mentioned; in fact, it does not lie on the terrain of this world at all. The priest is concerned about something in man that reaches into a higher world, in short, about man's immortal soul and its supernatural destiny.

However, not even the soul as such, not the soul as the determining and animating form in man or as an essential constituent of his nature, falls within the province of the pastoral ministry. Educational instruction, training, and guidance are also concerned with the soul, to the end that its development may mold the entire man, his character and his personality. Even when the term "soul-culture" is occasionally used in this connection, it does not mean and does not profess to mean the cure of souls in the pastoral sense. We come closer to the domain and the specific object of the pastoral ministry, the more we rule out everything that does not serve the higher interests of the soul of man.

Now, where exactly does the work of the priest, the so-called cure of souls, begin? At the point where the supernatural interests of the soul begin, that is, where natural and this-worldly considerations are no longer involved, but where there is question solely of the eternal destiny of the

[3] Heb. 5: 1.

human soul. This sphere of the soul is a field that must be tilled and sown by the consecrated hands of the priest, not by lay workers. At first glance, it may appear to be a small and sharply limited field, but, to change the figure, it resembles rather a burning focal-point, sending out its rays in every direction.

The heart and center of all Catholic pastoral activity is, therefore, nothing less than the eternal, supernatural welfare of man's soul. To prepare the soul for its supernatural goal, its true goal in life, that is, the blessed union with God throughout eternity, is the task of the priest. And so, from the beginning, the cure of souls has meant to rescue souls from the misery of sin, to protect them from further danger and contamination, and to lead them to the heights of virtue. Everything else that the priest undertakes must remain subordinated to this first duty of his vocation and has significance and value only in so far as it contributes to the discharge of this, his primary task.

2. To be sure, the pastoral ministry of today makes far greater demands upon the Catholic priest than ever before. The number of organizations and other external aids that in the course of time have been made to serve the ends of the ministry is almost unlimited. In the vast Catholic Church, changing conditions of time and place and nationality have produced an enormous and almost gay variety of ways and means to approach the souls of men. Hence it is not true, especially today, that the shepherd of souls can exercise his office in the peace and holy quiet of church and sacristy, far removed from the hurly-burly of daily life. These places, of course, are indispensable, but the priest cannot possibly confine his labors to them. The ministry reaches

out and touches a multitude of adjoining provinces which may not be overlooked or neglected without harm to the cure of souls.

To mention only the most important of these abutting provinces, we have education, art, literature, science, industry, commerce, economics, and politics. How foreign they all seem to the specific tasks of the priesthood, and especially of the pastoral ministry; and yet, how closely, both directly and indirectly, and how inseparably they are entwined with the work of the priesthood! Therefore the priest engaged in the cure of souls may not and cannot gaze indifferently and with folded arms at the activity in these various domains of public life. He has a lively interest therein; first, negative, to avert any dangers to the soul and the pastoral ministry that may arise from them; and then, positive, to enlist in the service of the ministry the forces for good that emanate from these different profane fields. Hence the Church is concerned about very many things that per se lie outside her province; she is concerned about them not for the sake of the things themselves, but solely from supernatural motives, and specifically because of her interest in the care and salvation of souls.

The Church herself, the priesthood as a whole, and the individual priest have of course the grave duty not to lose themselves in these temporal and outlying domains, lest they fall a prey to the danger of secularism; rather, they must always keep before their eyes the other-worldly nature and the divine mission of their vocation. The individual priest in particular must bear these truths in mind. Overladen, as he is, with the burdens and cares of the present-day ministry, the many external and earthly interests with which he is compelled to busy himself may otherwise cause him to lose sight of the essential and supernatural goal of his ministry. He must keep the essential purpose of his mission before his eyes to escape also another danger: excessive concern about externals in the cure of souls may lead him to neglect his own soul. The solemn words of St. Paul should act as a salutary warning: "I chastise my body, and bring it into subjection: lest perhaps, when I have preached to others, I myself should become a castaway." [4]

3. To stimulate a deeper understanding of the significance of the pastoral ministry to which he intends to dedicate himself, and to help him acquire even a faint appreciation of its necessity and excellence, we will in this place single out another point for consideration. The ministry is rightly called the most sublime and noblest work imaginable. The frequently quoted words of Dionysius the pseudo-Areopagite may well serve as the *leitmotif* in all pastoral activity: "Of all divine things the most divine is to co-operate with God for the salvation of souls." [5] Familiar also is the utterance of the Church father, St. Gregory Nazianzen: "The art of all arts, the science of all sciences, is to guide and rule men." [6]

---

[4] See I Cor. 9: 27.

[5] *De cael. hierarchia*, cap. 3 (*PG*, III, 165). *Omnium divinorum divinissimum est cooperari Deo ad salutem animarum.* This beautiful and often quoted sentence (which goes back to I Cor. 3: 9 and III John 1: 8) is not literally contained in the passage referred to. The complete text is as follows: *Etenim cuiuslibet eorum, qui sacrum ordinem sortiti sunt, in hoc sita perfectio est, ut ad divinam, pro captu quisque suo, promoveatur imitationem, quodque divinius est omnium, ipsius etiam Dei, ut Eloquia loquuntur, cooperator existat, divinamque in semetipso demonstret operationem, quoad potest, elucentem.* However, the sense of the passage is in complete agreement with the shorter quotation.

[6] *De fuga*, cap. 16 (*PG*, XXXV, 425).

We must proceed from a consideration of the greatness and worth that each human soul possesses in the order of nature and in the order of supernature, that we may acquire an understanding of the greatness and excellence of the pastoral ministry.

Is it an exaggeration to say that even in the natural order nothing in the world approaches a human soul in value? [7] As a matter of fact, when man is regarded as the crown of the whole visible creation, this is mainly because of the soul which he carries within him and which makes him tower high above all the other living things of earth. For this soul of his is a spirit, not fashioned from the stuff of earth but from the breath of God, imperishable, immortal. While the material world as a whole is only a dark and weak reflection of its divine Maker, the soul of man on the basis of its spirituality and immortality approaches the essence of the absolute and eternal Spirit of God, so that even by virtue of its natural endowment it may with perfect justice be spoken of as the image of God. Immortality connotes something inconceivably great. "Heaven and earth shall pass, but my words shall not pass," [8] our Lord in the full consciousness of His Messianic dignity once asserted. And neither shall the soul of man pass. When heaven and earth shall have come to an end, the Son of man will return as judge, and all the immortal souls of men will be compelled to appear before His judgment seat to hear their eternal fate.

4. However, the priest as shepherd of souls is concerned not so much about the natural worth of the soul as about

---

[7] Cf., for example, St. Jerome, *Hom. 3 in I Cor.* (*PG, LXI, 29*).
[8] Matt. 24: 35.

its supernatural value. By the grace of God the soul of man has been elevated to the supernatural order, which soars far above that of nature; and the priest as the "dispenser of the mysteries of God" is usually the one who unlocks the door leading to this higher order. The soul in the radiance and beauty of supernature is the most sublime work ever produced by the omnipotence and goodness of God. Faith teaches us that the soul, by means of sanctifying grace, receives a new and divine form of existence and life, by which men, according to the expression contained in the Second Epistle of St. Peter, become "partakers of the divine nature." [9] This is not the place for a disquisition on the glories of grace in the soul of man. We merely point out again that the priest as shepherd of souls has the sacred and lofty task of mediating this glory to the soul, of guarding and protecting it with loving care, and of laboring ever to increase it. He resembles the keeper of a holy temple, the custodian of a heavenly treasure. His also is the duty of helping to restore the sanctuary of the soul when sin has ravaged it, and to re-establish the kingdom of God that the sinner has wantonly destroyed in his soul. All these sublime services constitute pastoral care in the best and truest sense of the words, a real co-operation with God Himself against the powers of darkness. As a shining motto above this phase of the ministry, the saving of souls from destruction, are written the words of the Lord: "For what doth it profit a man, if he gain the whole world, and suffer the loss of his own soul?" [10]

The supernatural worth of the soul is brought home to

[9] See II Pet. 1: 4.
[10] Matt. 16: 26.

us still more graphically when we reflect upon what God Himself has done for the salvation of mankind. Ultimately all the works of divine omnipotence, wisdom, and love have the salvation of souls as their final aim. The incarnation, life, suffering, and death of the Son of God served this purpose alone. The establishment and organization of the Church, and the divine economy of salvation that is finding its fulfilment through the Church, have the *salus animarum* as their goal.

The priest's vocation and labor tend in the same direction. As St. Paul puts it, he is a coadjutor of God.[11] His task consists in helping God to carry out the most divine of all divine works, the salvation of souls. An *opus Dei* is what St. Paul called the vocational labor of himself and his disciple Timothy: "He worketh the work of the Lord, as I also do." [12]

Every priest as a shepherd of souls is filled with the uplifting and inspiring conviction that he is co-operating in the noblest of divine operations. This holy partnership with God should make him feel very humble, but at the same time happy and confident.

5. The conscientious pastor of souls stands in need of such a sustaining conviction, such a glad confidence. The ministry, noble and divine though it is, bristles with many external difficulties and furnishes occasion for countless sacrifices. To these are added the disillusionments, the discouragements, the depressed moods, and the feelings almost akin to despair, that oppress the heart of almost every shepherd of souls at some time or other. Precisely in our day,

[11] See I Cor. 3: 9.
[12] *Ibid.*, 16: 10.

the ministry is truly the art of all arts, that is, the most difficult and the most laborious of all, as the daily experience of every priest engaged in the cure of souls amply confirms. Incomparable are the joys of the ministry, but great also are the painful features and the worries connected with it. Today as heretofore, the ministry is undoubtedly the vocation that demands the most sacrifices and the greatest personal surrender on the part of those who are called to practice it. Bishop Dupanloup once wrote: "Man is the great means used by God for the saving of men. Such a mission is undeniably the greatest distinction that God can confer upon a person here below." But then he added: "This distinction is almost always purchased with pain, even with blood. One can save men only by sacrificing one's self, and often only by dying for them. Many times they do not want to be saved; then one must save them against their will, one must die for and through them." [18]

This observation of a noted educator expresses the ideal of the pastoral ministry and, at the same time, points to the tremendous difficulties that so often confront the real pastor of souls. Nor need this state of affairs surprise us. When our Lord sent out the first ministers, His Apostles, He warned them of the bitter experiences awaiting them. From His day to ours, this blending of happiness and sorrow has been the lot of the priesthood, particularly of the pastoral ministry, in every age. Not even the all-embracing, supremely unselfish ministry of the incarnate Son of God Himself, the greatest of pastors, was immune from this fate. When He hung dying on the cross, must not the world

[18] *Die Erziehung* (Ger. Transl.), I, 12.

have received the impression that all His redemptive and pastoral labor had ended in tragic bankruptcy, that His life and mission had been a complete failure? And yet, what in the eyes of the world seemed to be death and ruin was in reality the unfailing fountain source of a new life.

Christ's own ministry, which ended in cruel suffering and shameful death, constituted the basis for the eternal glorification of His human nature. "Ought not Christ to have suffered these things, and so to enter into his glory?" [14] was the question put by the Master to the uncomprehending disciples on the road to Emmaus. And what did St. Paul say of Him? "He humbled himself, becoming obedient unto death, even to the death of the cross. For which cause God also hath exalted him, and hath given him a name which is above all names: that in the name of Jesus every knee should bow, of those that are in heaven, on earth, and under the earth: and that every tongue should confess that the Lord Jesus Christ is in the glory of God the Father." [15] This, then, is the glorious and eternal reward that has come to the God-man for His work of redemption, for all the labors and sacrifices which He endured for the salvation of the souls of men.

6. The follower of Christ in the priesthood and in the ministry will not be without a similar reward in heaven. Consoling and full of hope is the assurance given by St. Peter to the bishops and priests of his day: "And when the prince of pastors shall appear, you shall receive a never fading crown of glory." [16] It is the same glory promised by

[14] Luke 24: 26.
[15] Phil. 2: 8–11.
[16] See I Pet. 5: 4.

the prophet of the Old Testament under another but similar figure: "But they that are learned shall shine as the brightness of the firmament: and they that instruct many to justice, as stars for all eternity." [17] The glory of the crown and the brilliance of the stars—such are the bold and glorious symbols employed by Holy Writ to make graphic the heavenly reward awaiting the faithful pastor of souls. Of course, the thought of recompense must not be the final or compelling motive in pastoral activity, or, for that matter, in any other moral act. Stronger and nobler motives are contained in the good work itself, in the superlative moral excellence of the cure of souls. Nevertheless, the thought of a superabundant reward in the next world, a reward that will come from the hand of Christ Himself, is also good and should not be rejected as less worthy; the firm hope of reward from God, which after all is a divine virtue, has nothing in common with the contemptible mercenary spirit that poisons and destroys any good action.

We can easily understand how the pastoral aspect of the priesthood will be exceptionally strong in its appeal to a young man filled with religious fervor and love for his fellow-man. The thought that he will one day be able to co-operate in the work of bringing relief to the people in their religious and moral needs, that as a priest he will be allowed to serve humanity, in the highest sense of that phrase, is often the healthy root from which a priestly vocation sprouts. To use the figures employed by our Lord, the greatness of the harvest and the paucity of laborers often make such an impression upon the heart of a high-minded youth that he feels compelled to enter the vineyard and

[17] Dan. 12: 3.

become a "coadjutor of God." Without doubt, such a motive, springing from a love for the pastoral ministry, is well adapted and fully able to sustain a priestly vocation with all its cares and sacrifices. However, the candidate must learn very early to purify and deepen, in the light of faith, all his love for mankind and the cure of souls.

Whoever wishes to become a Catholic priest and a pastor of souls must keep his eye focused upon man's supernatural need of salvation, and must let himself be guided by supernatural considerations. God and the soul, eternity and immortality, everlasting salvation and eternal damnation—these are the fundamental thoughts that must form the basis of his decision to dedicate himself to the ministry. When such motivation is evidently present, the step into the apostolic office may be taken without fear or hesitation, for then surely the call of God is at hand.

CHAPTER VII

The Priesthood and the World

I. TENSION AND OPPOSITION

1. Two sentences of the New Testament concerning the world seem to be contradictory and, what is the more remarkable, both come from the pen of the same Evangelist. The first sentence reads as follows: "For God so loved the world, as to give his only begotten Son; that whosoever believeth in him, may not perish, but may have life everlasting." [1] The other sentence is this: "Love not the world, nor the things which are in the world. If any man love the world, the charity of the Father is not in him. For all that is in the world, is the concupiscence of the flesh, and the concupiscence of the eyes, and the pride of life, which is not of the Father, but is of the world." [2] Since God loves the world with an extraordinary affection, why should we not love the world? Why should the Christian be obliged to deny the world his love? Why should he be expected deliberately to hold himself aloof from contact with it?

And what should be the attitude of the priest who, like Christ, has been sent into the world? Should he love the

[1] John 3: 16.
[2] See I John 2: 15 f.

world in the meaning of the first quotation, or should he hate it and turn away from it? Understood in the right sense, he should do neither to the exclusion of the other; rather, he should combine the two. Nor will the result be discord and division in his own soul. The priest loves the world and its inhabitants from the loftiest possible motive, he loves the immortal souls of men; and we have seen that as pastor of souls he is the truest lover and friend of mankind. His heart beats for the world; he loves it with a divine love, in order that he may win it for God.

Such is the one side of the picture. What about the other? The world is to be shunned, avoided, even hated, because it "is seated in wickedness," [3] because it is full of sin, sinful lusts, sinful dangers, and because the prince of this world is the archenemy of God.[4] Holy Writ contains numerous passages warning us against association and friendship with a world that is so hostile to God and so enmeshed in sin. This is the world of which Christ said that it pursues Him and His disciples with hatred, because they are not of it; [5] this is the world whose wisdom St. Paul called foolishness.[6]

Hence the world has a double aspect and deserves love or hatred according to the viewpoint from which it is regarded. Thus the apparent contradiction contained in the cited Scriptural passages receives a natural and satisfactory solution.

In the preceding chapter we spoke at length of the pastoral love that the priest has for the world. In the present chapter we again treat of the priest and the world; but

---

[3] *Ibid.*, 5: 19.
[4] John 12: 31.
[5] *Ibid.*, 15: 18 f.
[6] See I Cor. 3: 19.

now we are concerned with the reverse side of the relationship, the side that is expressed by the words, repudiation of the world and renunciation of the world. The ideas contained in these phrases indicate that the priest, while fully sharing God's devoted love for the world, must at the same time oppose and reject the world. Loneliness, misunderstanding, hatred, and persecution will always be the lot of the Catholic priest in a world that is estranged from God.

2. Nor can it be otherwise. For repudiation of the world is an essential constitutent of genuine Christianity and *a fortiori* of the Catholic priesthood. This is the first point that must here be stressed. When Christ stood in the praetorium of the Roman procurator and was questioned about His kingship, He explained that He was in truth a king, but that His kingdom was not of this world.[7] By this statement He wished to express, first of all, that the Messianic kingdom of which He is the head differs entirely in nature, trend, and aim from the earthly political realms of mundane rulers and that therefore the Roman Empire had nothing to fear from Him. But we can detect another thought expressed in an undertone, as it were, by our Lord's, words, namely, that His kingdom stands in basic opposition to the world in so far as its foundations and purposes are opposed to the kingdoms of the world.

And such, indeed, is the fact. Between Christ's kingdom and kingship, that is, the Christian religion, and what is called "the world," there exists an abysmal difference, a difference that is not only neutral and negative, but one that has produced grave tension and mutual opposition from the very beginning. Harmony and peace between the

[7] John 18: 36.

kingdom of God and the kingdom of the world are a dimly glimpsed and remote ideal, one that can be achieved only if the world submits without reservation or qualification to the kingdom of Christ. Our Lord Himself foretold that this contradiction would last until the end of time; hence for us there can be question only of a more or less successful approach to the ideal.

At one time it seemed as though some sort of reconciliation and harmony between the two great powers, the Church and the world, had been achieved. When at the height of the Middle Ages an Innocent III sat in the chair of Peter and dominated the entire West, many of his contemporaries undoubtedly thought that the supremacy of Christ's kingdom had at last been permanently assured, that the conflict between the *civitas Dei* and the *civitas terrestris* had disappeared forever. But, to begin with, the vision of Innocent's contemporaries was limited by a too narrow horizon, since they regarded the comparatively insignificant West as the whole world. Besides, many ideas then prevalent regarding ecclesiastical domination in the political field revealed a misconception and perversion of the real purpose of the Church and her mission; this fact was recognized by the best and most spiritual minds of that time, notably by St. Francis of Assisi. In addition, history has shown that the Church's supremacy in civil affairs was only a beautiful dream which soon dissolved into nothingness. A sharp decline followed this golden age of the papacy's political power, and in the course of the succeeding centuries an unhappy struggle between the spiritual and the civil power developed.

The conflict between Christianity and the world is ineradicable, both in public and in private life. In the microcosm of the individual we also find disagreement, friction, and conflict between the power of God and the powers of the world. Christianity teaches us that the deep-lying cause of these tragic phenomena is the disastrous lack of harmony in human nature, with its roots in original sin, the ancient guilt of mankind. The consequences and effects of that sin have produced what in Biblical language is called "the world," and constitute the opposition to God and Christianity.

Hence the conquest of the world, which the divine Founder of Christianity inscribed on the standard of His Church as its program, can consist in nothing else but renunciation and rejection of the world. That the priest-hood, in which the content and the aims of Christianity receive their most forceful expression, is compelled to take this attitude toward the world, needs no further proof. Re-nunciation of the world does not mean simply flight from the world, such as has been practiced in all ages by those who pursue monastic ideals. Retreat from the world in this strict sense can in the very nature of things be the duty of only a few, and least of all, as we have already pointed out, can it be the obligation of the secular priest.

But flight from the world can also be understood in a moral sense, namely, as flight from worldly dispositions and worldly ways of thought, from the sensual life and the sin-ful activity of the world. Understood in this higher sense, flight from the world means renunciation of the world and is without doubt the general duty of all Christians. We must be able to face the situation squarely, looking at things as they are and recognizing the existence of the conflict; we must never try to banish the contradictions between the world and Christianity by making false compromises and improper concessions. Attempts of this nature are doomed to failure from the start and always bring with them the grave danger that the essential points of Christian faith will be thereby distorted and weakened. Christianity demands clear thinking and an unequivocal attitude in dogmatic as well as in moral and ascetic questions; it tolerates no softening or distortion of the truth.

The priest and the aspirant to the priesthood must clearly grasp this necessary attitude which they are obliged to assume toward the world. The ecclesiastical designation *clerus, clericus,* expresses the truth that the priest's lot is cast with God, and not with the world. "In the full bloom of youth he has died in the midst of the world, since his heart no longer belongs to the world, his hopes and desires are no longer concerned with it. Yes, dead; but only that part of him which was low and earthly and transitory has died." [8] The seminarian must never forget that the ideal and eternal model of the Catholic priesthood is not an earthly king with crown and scepter, not a king friendly to the world, but the suffering, self-immolating Son of God who renounced and overcame the world.

3. Renunciation of the world and the idea of sacrifice have held first place in priestly vocation since the days when Christ gave His example. Hettinger writes: "Christ redeemed the world in two ways: He died for our sins and He rose again for our justification (Rom. 4: 25). Hence the priesthood necessarily bears a double stamp, one of death and the other of life. . . . Dying to the world, living

[8] Hettinger, *Timotheus* (1909), p. 52.

for Christ—such is the vocation and the life of the priest." [9]
Sacrifice in the sense of personal immolation for mankind
and of heroic renunciation of the possessions and pleasures
of the world, aye, of profound contempt for the world, such
as manifested by Christ during His sojourn on earth, give
the priesthood its unique character. The appallingly sublime
sacrifice that He offered while dying on the cross not only
constituted the greatest act and achievement of His own
priestly life, but breathed His spirit into the Catholic priesthood for all time, so that priesthood and the idea of sacrifice can nevermore be separated from each other. The
Catholic priest is confronted daily by altar and cross in the
performance of his liturgical functions; they have a symbolic meaning for the whole trend of his spiritual and
priestly life. Whoever does not love the cross and sacrifice,
whoever shrinks from renunciation and denial as far as the
world is concerned, had better give up all idea of becoming a priest of God.

2. MEANING AND PURPOSE OF THE PRIEST'S RENUNCIATION OF THE WORLD

Where are we to look for the meaning of the Christian
terms: renunciation of the world, conquest of self, mortification, and sacrifice? Have these phrases any meaning
at all?

1. The naturalistic person whose whole way of thought
is limited by the earthly and the this-worldly would
promptly answer: No. He simply does not understand these
terms, nor is he able to understand them, because his out-

[9] *Loc. cit.*, pp. 51 f.

look is totally different and, besides, he does not possess the spiritual faculty that would enable him to grasp these ideas. And the person who groans under the tyranny of untamed passions and lusts, whose lower nature instinctively flares up in rebellion when spiritual demands are made upon it, not only has no understanding for these ideas, but even combats them with a personal hostility. Nor can we expect any understanding of these concepts on the part of a young man who is bubbling over with exuberant vital energy and who approves the principle that life should be lived to the full, who feels that he must provide satisfaction for all the lusts and urges of his animal nature. Of course, it often happens that, in the remorseful hours which follow disillusioning experiences, the meaning of a different way of life may begin to dawn, like a light from a better world, upon such an old or young sensualist.

Far more happy is the situation in which many another finds himself. The world of thought proper to a person of this type has been saturated from childhood with Christian ideas and principles; his training and education have been determined by Christian standards. The Catholic priest usually has such a wholesome family background, and from the beginning has had a practical acquaintance with the fundamental concepts of renunciation and sacrifice. From earliest years he learned to know and apply self-discipline in the struggle against self-indulgence.

2. The assumption that forms the basis of Christian morality is the fundamental teaching of Christianity that man, as a result of original sin, appears to be a dual being; on the one hand he is dragged downward to the low level of the sensual and the animal, on the other hand he is im-

pelled upward toward the ideal world of the good, the true, and the noble. The Apostle St. Paul learnt by personal experience to recognize this double nature in himself, and gives classical expression to this fact in his ethical teaching. In the well-known passage of his Epistle to the Romans he speaks of the double law that he feels in his members: the law of the mind, which gives him pleasure in the law of God; and the law of evil, fighting against the former and captivating him in the law of sin that is in his members.[10] On the basis of these opposing tendencies he notes a two-fold man: the sensual, carnal man (*homo animalis, carnalis*), and the higher, spiritual man (*homo spiritualis, caelestis*).[11]

The universal fact that such an internal division exists in the heart of man is beyond question. The young seminarian who becomes aware of it for the first time in his own spiritual life should not be startled or ashamed. The awakening in his breast of these low impulses, the very existence of which he perhaps did not even suspect, may at first cause him painful disillusionment, making him uneasy and shattering the beautiful dream that he had regarded as reality. This is the more likely to be the case if the happiness of an unsullied innocence has reigned over his childhood and early youth. However, after this first awakening of his lower instincts and appetites, he will realize more clearly that for him, too, a moral life means struggle and self-control. He now has a clear view of the enemy against whom he must battle. It is the demon of his own many-shaped concupiscence, stealthily approaching his youthful

---

[10] Rom. 7: 21–23.
[11] Cf. Rom. 7: 14; I Cor. 2: 14 f.; 15: 47.

heart in the form of concupiscence of the eyes, concupiscence of the flesh, and pride of life.

The watchword is: *Abstine!* Experience confirms the truth that this terrible enemy which man carries within himself can be overcome in no other way than by self-denial and mortification. Any attempt to conquer him by occasional concessions and by conciliation has always proved itself to be futile.

3. NECESSITY OF RENUNCIATION OF SELF AND OF THE WORLD

1. The small but powerful world of a person's own corrupted nature must be renounced; its demands urging to sin must not be satisfied, but must be ruthlessly denied and rejected. In the struggle with the inner world of evil, at times a harsh attack against one's own self or a vigorous and perhaps painful throttling of one's own nature is unavoidable. This is a fundamental doctrine of Christianity. The stern language used by our Lord when speaking of scandal applies here also: "And if thy right eye scandalize thee, pluck it out and cast it from thee. For it is expedient for thee that one of thy members should perish, rather than that thy whole body be cast into hell. And if thy right hand scandalize thee, cut it off, and cast it from thee: for it is expedient for thee that one of thy members should perish, rather than that thy whole body go into hell." [12]

Wherever the Christian religion is taken seriously, these almost brutal sounding words of Christ are well understood. And no one grasps them better than the priest, whose

[12] Matt. 5: 29 f.

pastoral eye gazes upon so much spiritual distress and corruption.

The unaided human will is able only in rare instances to summon up the courage and strength needed for the decisions of renunciation in regard to a person's own inner world; such instances are so infrequent that we need not consider them at all. Generally the will is too weak for the task, even when it musters all its natural powers. If such renunciation is to be successful, that is, if it is to result in thoroughgoing self-denial and unceasing self-discipline, the assistance of divine grace is unconditionally necessary.

2. Next to the little world of our own ego stands the great world about us, the world of external things and of men; in regard to this world also the priest has the duty of renunciation. The complimentary testimony that our Lord bore to the Apostles in His sacerdotal prayer, "They are not of the world, as I also am not of the world," [13] must always be fully true of every Catholic priest. His mission indeed takes him into the world, and his duty obliges him to live in the midst of men. He must do so, however, not that he may live in the world in a worldly manner, but that he may convert the world to God. *Instaurare omnia in Christo* [14] is the heavenly motto that must remain the inspiration of all priestly labor in the world.

The term "the world" has a double meaning. The world, consisting of heaven and earth, the world created by God for His external glory and the good of man, is a marvel of divine omnipotence and wisdom; it bears the mark of its divine Maker; and the more deeply the mind of man pene-

[13] John 17: 16.
[14] Eph. 1: 10.

trates into its mysteries, the more clearly are its majesty
and beauty revealed. The royal psalmist in the Old Testament justly sang of this cosmos: "The heavens show forth the
glory of God, and the firmament declareth the work of his
hands." [15] For the Christian, too, the world in this sense is
an object of joy and love, not of contempt, much less of
hatred.

But another kind of world exists. We spoke of it at the
beginning of the present chapter. It is the world that has
turned away from God and is actively hostile to Him, the
world that rejects Christ and His Gospel, the world that
believes it can get along without Christ and without God.
Its goal is a purely earthly culture, the refinement of life
with earthly pleasures and values, the material, economic,
and cultural uplift of mankind, and all this to the exclusion
of an eternal, supernatural destiny. Whether we call the
"religion" of the world materialism or humanitarianism
makes not the slightest difference; its essence consists in
opposition to the religion of Christ.

The priest, as the servant of Christ and of the Church,
may never waver in his attitude toward this world. The
abstine which he must pronounce with regard to his own
sensual nature must also be spoken here. It is of paramount
importance that the priest who, as the ambassador of Christ,
is sent out into the world by the Church does not himself
become worldly as a result of his close asssociation with the
world, its ideas, viewpoints, strivings, and works.

To make the clergy worldly is the aim upon which the
avowed enemies of the Church and its secret enemies always set their heart. The foes of the Church have met with

[15] Ps. 18: 2.

little success in their efforts at the secularization, that is, the alienation of Church property. The result of such attempts has been to free the Church and to make her more mobile for her specific spiritual tasks. Far more dangerous would be the secularization of the clergy itself, of its whole attitude toward life and its entire manner of thought. The periods of so-called enlightenment, when such attempts achieved a partial success, serve as a warning and engender the hope that such times may never recur.

The "man of God" must remain what he is; he may not become a man of the world. If this were to happen, his priesthood would be undermined and his mission rendered fruitless. Worldly priests are no blessing to the Church; they bring no honor to their vocation and no happiness to themselves. They are lamentable phenomena, men suffering from internal division, nor do they find peace of soul and satisfaction where they hope to find it, namely, in union with the world. "No man can serve two masters." [16] This word of the Lord applies particularly to the priest who tries to be spiritual and worldly at the same time. Ultimately the world itself will usually draw back from the man who comes to it in the garb of a priest and tries to think and act with her, but who cannot do so without going to pieces internally. In the end such a person loses the confidence and respect of even his presumed worldly friends, because the false and muddled nature of his character cannot remain hidden from them in the long run.

Consequently the embryo priest must be on his guard lest he become infected with worldly ideas and principles. As a rule the good seminarian has, one might almost say, an

[16] Matt. 6: 24.

inborn weather sense for what is worldly, for what is all too worldly, and for what will not harmonize properly with his vocation. The mind of a candidate for the priesthood should of course be open and unprejudiced, but he must not absorb anything of the worldly spirit or attitude, anything that his theological instinct at once senses as foreign and inimical to the spirit of his calling.

3. Precisely for that reason he must exercise great caution with regard to the reading and study of books that are hostile to the Church and religion, and also the works of so-called liberal authors. The ecclesiastical prohibition of books, the primary object of which is to preserve the purity of faith and morals, has in the case of the seminarian the added purpose of shielding his vocation. He should appreciate the pedagogic value of the Church's ban on dangerous reading and should regard the pertinent regulations as something natural and matter of course. Never should he consider them as a form of unwarranted guardianship and of intellectual bondage, but rather as a salutary warning intended to protect him from the insidious poison of ideas and principles that are unchurchly and worldly, if not actually destructive of vocation. In the guise of legitimate intellectual curiosity and of scientific research, such wrong notions all too easily find lodgment in the mind of a young man athirst for knowledge. The result is confusion in his inner world of thought and conviction. The toying with all kinds of so-called liberal ideas destroys the clarity and certainty he must have regarding his vocation, and makes thinking with the Church almost impossible. The mind of such a young man is still too immature; it lacks the training and discipline necessary to separate at a glance the wheat

from the chaff. A worldly attitude gradually takes the place of his former tender ecclesiastical sense; when a person's inner world has fallen a prey to such secularization, the external effect upon his life and vocation follows as a natural consequence. These reflections should convince the seminarian that his vocation places upon him the strict obligation of avoiding such worldly influences and of protecting himself from such liberalizing tendencies.

Moreover, that abstention from purely worldly pleasures and forms of amusement must be practiced by seminarian and priest need only be briefly noted in this place. Much that the world of today offers in the way of cultural and recreational pleasure is not suited for priests, even though members of other callings may indulge in them without harm or scandal. No one expects the seminarian or the priest to be a sullen killjoy who feels he must go through life in a spirit of brooding melancholy. Certainly not that. The priest's heart also has a right to joy, a right to pleasure in nature and in human life, and he should consciously promote and satisfy this legitimate craving as a refreshment and a comfort to his soul. But it must be a noble, pure joy that he seeks, a pleasure without admixture of evil. Thanks be to God, there are many sources from which such unclouded pleasures and joys flow in abundance, many in the bosom of nature itself.[17]

Moderation and unpretentiousness befit the priest with regard to material possessions, and these virtues are urgently recommended for his personal way of life and the domestic arrangements of his dwelling place. Simplicity should be

[17] In this connection see Bishop Keppler's beautiful book, *More Joy* (1914).

the first law. Everything that smacks of luxury and worldliness must be kept far from the home of a priest. Unlike the religious, the secular priest takes no vow of poverty, and this circumstance leaves him greater freedom in the matter of earthly possessions. However, it does not release him from the general duty of every priest, even of every Christian, of being detached in his heart from riches as such, of being free from all inordinate attachment to earthly goods, and of fostering in his heart a genuine love for poverty. The rectory and the domestic arrangements of the priest should be modest and in good taste. His home should not be a hovel, but certainly a house from which everything soft and effeminate has been banished. And if it comes to that, a humble cottage would be far more suited to the priest than a pretentious mansion.

4. DEEPER MOTIVATION FOR RENUNCIATION OF THE WORLD

1. We need not look far to find an authoritative basis for the denial of self and of the world that is demanded of the Christian, and specifically of the priest. It is contained in the clearest possible manner in the teaching and example of Christ Himself. The following quotation is pertinent: "In the life of Jesus we find many indications of friendliness for the world, so that we may conclude that the Lord was no enemy of the world on principle. Nor could He be, since the world was the creation of His Father and the stage on which His love was manifested and His heroic deeds performed." [18] But in the last analysis, as the same author points out in the passage that follows, this love of our Lord

[18] Rademacher, *Religion und Leben* (1929), p. 205.

for the world is to be understood only in the sense of a conquest and a renewal of the world. Jesus condemned the world in the form in which He found it; He despised and avoided it, warning His disciples against it and its works. We cannot escape the conclusion that the following of Christ, as taught by the Gospel, has as its basis a renunciation of the world and consistent denial of self. The entire Sermon on the Mount bears testimony to this. Indicative of the whole ethical system propounded by Christ are the words: "If any man will come after me, let him deny himself, and take up his cross, and follow me." [19] Such self-denial demands a corresponding renunciation and a more than ordinary denial of the world.

Our Lord's own life and actions were fully in accord with His teaching and with the demands He made upon His followers. He was speaking with full truth and without exaggeration when He asserted: "The foxes have holes, the birds of the air nests: but the Son of man hath not where to lay his head." [20] Such indeed was the aspect of His life on earth. He really had no home, no permanent dwelling place. At times alone, at times accompanied by His disciples, He journeyed through the length and breadth of Palestine, going from city to city, from village to village, without rest, without home, without possessions. He endured the self-imposed lot of absolute poverty with divinely happy composure and unconcern; He loved it and recommended it to His own for imitation. He, the infinitely wealthy One, to whom all power in heaven and in earth had been given, emptied Himself to the extreme of privation and want. In

[19] Matt. 16: 24.
[20] *Ibid.*, 8: 20.

poverty He entered the world, in poverty He passed His days on earth, and in poverty He took His departure from this world, leaving behind Him no earthly possessions. He did all this of His own free will, under no compulsion of nature or circumstances, and with the intention of giving His own, above all His disciples, an unmistakable and shining example and a correct philosophy of life. Solemn and stern, but also full of the consciousness of His Messianic vocation, are the words in which He expressed His fundamental attitude toward His closest blood relations: "Who is my mother and who are my brethren? . . . Whosoever shall do the will of my Father, that is in heaven, he is my brother, and sister, and mother." [21] Virginal and celibate, He denied Himself all the legitimate pleasures and consolations of family life. His love did not belong in first place to the few who were bound to Him by the natural ties of relationship, but to all whom He had come to redeem, and pre-eminently to those who had joined His entourage as disciples. His lofty soul always remained free of any sort of sensual attachment to individuals. Even the intimate friendship which He cultivated with Lazarus and his sisters in Bethany was entirely spiritual and noble in character, without the slightest trace of sensual emotion. In short, our Lord's entire life was dominated by the great idea of self-denial, of self-immolation for all.

And so the eternal High Priest confronts us as a priest to whom the sacrificial idea and the sacrificial act were the beacon, the guiding star of His vocation. How could anyone who wishes to follow Him in the priesthood disregard this essential feature in our Lord's conception of life and

[21] *Ibid.*, 12: 48, 50.

vocation? How can a priest lack the desire to absorb the same spirit of self-denial and world-renunciation?

2. The Church does not indeed require that a priest who lives in the world and who is not at the same time a member of one of the religious orders forego all possessions and every creature comfort. The fact that she has at no time imposed upon the secular priesthood the obligation of voluntary poverty shows that she has a profound appreciation of the peculiarity and the special needs of this vocation as distinct from the religious state. But the secular priest is not thereby relieved of the duty to refrain from amassing earthly treasure from the goods of the Church and the emoluments of his office. He, too, must live in accordance with St. Paul's admonition to Timothy: "But having food, and wherewith to be covered, with these we are content. . . . For the desire of money is the root of all evils." [22]

This trait of ascetic self-denial, together with the renunciation of all earthly goods, recurs regularly in the lives of all the great saints, clerical and lay, male and female, who as apt pupils followed in the footsteps of the Master. No one has ever become holy without such renunciation of self and of the world. Even the new age "saint," the "holy this-world person," as one author calls him,[23] will never be able to dispense with the feature of renunciation, in spite of all his readiness to make concessions to nature. Viewed outwardly, many saints appear almost to have surpassed their divine model in the way of mortification and rejection of the world. We need think only of the spiritual giants who flourished in the days of the hermits and of early

[22] See I Tim. 6: 8, 10.
[23] Rademacher, op. cit., p. 215.

monasticism. But even the others, holy priests and laymen, who did not forsake the world and repair to the solitude of the desert, died to themselves and the world and, to speak with St. Paul, lived "as having nothing, and possessing all things." [24] What the same Apostle truthfully said of himself, "I chastise my body, and bring it into subjection: lest perhaps, when I have preached to others, I myself should become a castaway," [25] was true also of many saintly bishops and priests in the centuries that followed St. Paul. Men whose austere self-denial and complete renunciation of the world fill us with amazement and awe, men like Augustine, Jerome, Francis of Assisi, Aloysius of Gonzaga, always exerted a profound influence upon their contemporaries.

That the priest is more urgently obligated to mortification, sacrifice, and asceticism than the average layman of the Church follows from the greater objective dignity and holiness of the priesthood and from the peculiar nature of its duties, particularly in the pastoral care of souls. Complete dedication to his vocation, celibacy, renunciation of family ties, are demands which the Church, at least in the Latin rite, makes upon her priests; they are demands that cannot be met without a corresponding measure of idealism and an unselfish spirit of sacrifice. The fact that the Church, in contrast to the Christian sects, dares to make such demands and to insist unswervingly and unflinchingly upon their fulfilment is an evidence of the inner moral power that the Church confidently attributes to herself and her priesthood.

[24] See II Cor. 6: 10.
[25] See I Cor. 9: 27.

The Catholic priesthood, therefore, is not for weak and effeminate souls, not for lackadaisical idlers who have not the spirit of sacrifice and the strength and energy necessary to despise the world and to practice mortification. Men in whom the ideal of the priesthood awakens no response will at best become mere clerical functionaries who, when things go well, fulfil their most necessary duties with external correctness. But they never become torch-bearers, never true men of God and the Church, who are on fire with zeal and animated with priestly enthusiasm. Today more than ever before, the Church needs priests who are anointed not only outwardly with the oil of the sacrament, but inwardly with the flaming power of the Holy Spirit, priests who are characterized by an unselfishness that wins men over and conquers the world. In contrast to these, priests who have become weary of their vocation, priests who are egotistical and self-seeking, are more of a liability than an asset to the kingdom of God on earth.

Persons who have such a jejune conception of priestly vocation, who can work up no enthusiasm for higher ideals, should never put their hand to the plow, that is, they should never entertain the idea of becoming priests. They are only deceiving themselves, and if nevertheless they succeed in obtaining holy orders, one is tempted to say, fraudulently, they will almost inevitably dishonor and compromise the priestly state.

Genuine priesthood, rightly understood and fully grasped, is not a commonplace or ordinary thing. Fundamentally it is something only for high-minded, ideal, and unselfish souls, souls able to renounce the world and the natural pleasures of the senses, not in a spirit of gloomy resentment, but willingly and with happy hearts, souls who regard the world with a contempt based not on arrogance but on confidence in victory, souls that have learned to discipline themselves.

The divinely called candidate to the sanctuary finds no difficulty in understanding the scene that once took place between Jesus, two of His disciples, and their mother. The mother of the sons of Zebedee brought them to our Lord and, with the proud feelings of a mother who had given Him both her sons, asked Him: "Say that these my two sons may sit, the one on thy right hand, and the other on thy left, in thy kingdom." Jesus understood perfectly the motive prompting this well-meant plea of the anxious mother, but He turned from her and looked earnestly at the two disciples; to them He said: "Can you drink of the chalice that I shall drink?" This question, unexpected by mother and sons alike, pointed to an entirely different conception of vocation than that held by the mother; it made clear to the two disciples an essential feature of their apostolic office. A hearty and determined *"possumus"* was their answer, and the Lord permitted them to remain at His side.[26]

Today as then, genuine disciples desiring to dedicate themselves to the service of a Master who faces them with the chalice in His hand and a question in His eyes, must also be able to answer: *Possumus,* we can.

3. What is the ultimate purpose and fruit of the denial of self and of the world that the priest is called upon to practice? Certainly not the somber melancholy of a soul that feels itself oppressed, chained, and enslaved, that be-

[26] Matt. 20: 20–23; see also Mark 10: 35–39.

lieves it must restrain all its energy. The fruit of all self-denial and renunciation of the world should be to raise and ennoble the spirit, to free the whole person from chains. True Christian freedom, the freedom of the children of God, is the lofty goal that self-control has in view and that is attainable in no other way. It is not the freedom of the man of untamed passions and urges, not the presumed freedom of the hedonist and man of the world who surrenders himself without restraint to the evil powers that emerge from the turbid depths of his animal nature. Such freedom is nothing but a miserable slavery, unworthy of a human being. Nor do we mean the freedom of the man of power and dominance who in his insane and overweening pride asserts only his own ego and would like to treat his fellow-men as slaves, as stepping-stones in his brutal lust for supremacy. Freedom of this sort is essentially foreign to the spirit of Christianity and of no value at all to the priest, the "man of God." Considered rightly, it is only a sham freedom, unable to make anyone really free and happy.

The ideal of true freedom, on the other hand, the freedom sponsored and demanded by Christianity, is found in the man who is inwardly free, the man who is master of himself and of his surrounding world, the man who walks willingly and with undisturbed calm along the road of morality and virtue to perfection. Such a one indeed remains bound by the moral law, but he does voluntarily and from an inner urge what the law commands and the moral order requires. For him the law is not a restraining and burdensome shackle, but simply a welcome spur toward good. He observes the laws of the moral order and obeys them willingly, not because of the law itself, not from purely formal reasons, but because he recognizes that ultimately the moral law is an emanation of the divine will and an aid to virtue and perfection. The ultimate goal that the morally free man strives after is God Himself, the final end of all creatures. While others are impeded on the way toward God by all kinds of obstacles and handicaps, the morally free man hastens along an open road leading directly to his final goal; he resembles an eagle who flies swiftly and unerringly to his mountain aerie.

But this divine freedom does not fall into a person's lap automatically and without labor. It is the noble reward that comes to a man for his struggle against self and the world; it is the priceless recompense for renunciation of the world and self-denial. This prize of victory more than outweighs all the labors and privations, all the sacrifices and acts of renunciation that it cost.

5. CONCLUSIONS FOR THE SEMINARIAN

1. The seminarian, and he particularly, must know and ponder all that has been said here about renunciation of the world and self-denial. From the very beginning he must recognize clearly that, in view of his future vocation, above all in view of the obligation of celibacy which is joined to that vocation, he must assume a much stricter attitude toward the world, toward himself, toward his own nature, than is required of another person of like age who has not the priesthood in mind. Even if he is led at times to imagine that his inner life resembles the smooth surface of a placid lake, he must still be convinced of the truth that this state

of affairs will not always perdure; violent internal storms are sure to break out sooner or later, since no one, as a rule, is spared such experiences. But the thing that will give him powerful protection in any eventual crisis is a healthy mistrust of himself and of the constancy of his own will, coupled with a strong reliance on the grace of God. "Unhappy man that I am," cried St. Paul in the midst of his struggles, "who shall deliver me from the body of this death?" But glancing upward with confidence, he himself gave the consoling answer: "The grace of God, by Jesus Christ our Lord." [27]

2. Two groups of candidates are found among the aspirants to the priesthood. In the first are those who are equipped from the outset with such a favorable and happy moral endowment that they experience hardly anything of the rift that exists in human nature, or they experience it very late, after they have advanced to riper and more stable years. A deeply religious home, a thoroughly Christian education, early habits of virtue, a morally wholesome environment—all these things have acted as a protecting dam to hold the waters of evil at a distance, and thus permit the seeds of virtue to develop undisturbed. They are the *animae candidae,* the unsullied souls that shine like burnished gold in the glory of purity and innocence. In many cases such fortunate young men have a natural inclination to the study of theology and the priesthood. Perhaps more than anything else, the virginal aspect of the sacerdotal state is an irresistible attraction to them. But, no matter how highly developed this natural predilection

[27] Rom. 7: 24 f.

for the priesthood may be, care must be taken precisely in the case of such candidates that they acquire no false illusions, that they allow no softness or false self-assurance to insinuate itself, and that they cultivate strong and manly traits of character. Later, when the violent battles start and the acts of renunciation required in the priesthood become difficult, they will then have sufficient stamina to withstand the assaults and to meet the test; they will enter the arena as well prepared warriors, armed with the weapons of the spirit and confident of victory.

Beside these fortunate children of nature and grace stand other young men who were denied the opportunity of growing up and developing in such favorable circumstances. At an early age the heavy burden of original sin pressed down upon their soul; strong sensual urges impeded their spiritual progress almost from the beginning. The battles between flesh and spirit set in early, and their lives have been a succession of victories and defeats. Only unceasing and energetic wrestling with self and continuous battling have finally led to mastery of their lower nature and a permanent victory of the spirit and of grace. Such young men, who have become accustomed to self-conquest and have learned by personal experience the necessity of making sacrifices, are certainly eligible for the priesthood, in fact, they are not the least desirable candidates.

However, when moral aptitudes are so inadequate and weak that complete victory over self remains doubtful, if not downright impossible, even after the greatest exertion, a priestly vocation can hardly live on, if it germinates at all. A certain measure of inherited good moral qualities, in addition to intellectual talent, constitutes an indispensable prerequisite for the birth and growth of priestly vocation.

3. In all circumstances the candidate, whether belonging to the first or to the second group, has the peremptory obligation to busy himself with the important work of moral and ascetic preparation while he pursues his technical studies. Mind and heart must be formed, educated, and trained with the same diligence and at the same time.

We intend to speak of the meaning and necessity of asceticism in more detail in another place. At this time we wish, however, to issue a short admonition; the seminarian must not shrink from moral exertion; he must not avoid self-conquest or dodge sacrifice. He must be no coward or weakling, stifling the heroic impulses that rise in his own breast. He must be convinced that Christ can use no such puny souls in His priesthood. He must take to heart the words of Thomas à Kempis: "The greater violence thou offerest to thyself, the greater progress thou shalt make." [28]

If the seminarian, supported by the grace of God, earnestly does battle with himself and strives incessantly to detach himself inwardly from the goods and pleasures of this world, in order that he may belong more completely to God and his holy vocation, he need have no fear that such asceticism will beget in him a spirit of resigned stoicism or of weary pessimism, or that he is expected to stifle all natural feelings of joy. On the contrary, he will resemble a happy, carefree child who gambols in the sunlight and finds delight in the pleasures and flowers of God's garden.

[28] *Imitation of Christ*, Bk. I, 25.

And so it is in reality. Renunciation of the world and of self, practiced from the loftiest motives, does not darken the eye or oppress the heart; on the contrary, it floods the soul with light and sunshine, with contentment and happiness. Self-control and detachment from worldly things make it possible for us to serve God cheerfully, as Holy Writ commands us to do: "Serve ye the Lord with gladness." [29] They also make it easy for us to understand the words of our Lord: "Take up my yoke upon you . . . , for my yoke is sweet and my burden light." [30]

The seminarian who plans to assume the honor and the burden of the priesthood should reflect often and seriously upon such words of Scripture, that he may be saturated with their significance. From them he will always draw courage and confidence in God, and the healthy optimism that is so indispensable for all pastoral and apostolic labor. They will imbue him with the certainty of victory and the sanguine disposition of Christ who, in spite of all disappointments and external failures, encouraged His disciples with the glad assurance: "Have confidence, I have overcome the world." [31]

[29] Ps. 99: 2.
[30] Matt. 11: 29 f.
[31] John 16: 33.

Chapter VIII

The Priesthood and the Priest

I. CLOSE CONNECTION

1. The priesthood unquestionably stands in closer relationship to the incumbent of this holy office than to any other person or thing. For the duration of his life the dignity and the burden of his vocation are the lot of the individual priest; for better or for worse he is wedded to the priesthood. No other calling so completely monopolizes the entire person of its members as does the Catholic priesthood. In the various mundane professions the possibility always is present that a person, failing in his efforts to establish a spiritual affinity between himself and his calling, can still fulfil the duties of his station in life in an outwardly correct manner, even though the inclination of his soul draws him to other ideals and aims that give more satisfaction to his heart. The link between such a person and his actual vocation is merely external and by virtue of his office; and his office or profession simply serves the purpose of providing him with a livelihood. With regard to ordinary secular callings this situation, while not ideal or desirable, is at least possible and endurable.

But an arrangement of this kind will simply not work

where the priesthood is concerned. The peculiar nature of the priestly office demands that its incumbents give more than merely a part of their available time or a part of their energy; it requires much more than a merely external interest and an outwardly correct fulfilment of duty. The priesthood calls for the complete dedication of the whole person; it engages all the faculties of mind and heart, of body and soul. A priest who is nothing but an official, a priest without a priestly heart, a priest who is not inwardly wedded to his vocation, would be a caricature, a moral impossibility. As far as he himself is concerned, he would suffer from internal discord, and inevitably would become in the end a profoundly unhappy man. Either a priest through and through, a priest with heart and soul, or not a priest at all—such must be the attitude of anyone who thinks of embracing this vocation. The words of the Lord, "No man can serve two masters," [1] apply with particular pertinence in this instance.

2. To avoid coming into such ruinous conflict with himself and with God, the candidate for the priestly office must dedicate himself to his vocation in such a way that he gives himself entirely and undividedly to his calling, reserving no part of his person and no place in his heart for the service of extraneous interests. We need not think necessarily of the sinful and degrading service of mammon, which is incompatible not only with the priesthood but with the faithful service of God in general. Even honorable pursuits that engross the heart and mind are incompatible with genuine priesthood, except when such service is essentially connected with the aims of priestly vocation,

[1] Matt. 6: 24.

as in the case of a Catholic scholar or educator; in such circumstances the activity, while not priestly in the strict sense, is nevertheless the outgrowth of a genuine priestly disposition. The heart remains priestly, and the avocation does not impair in the least the individual's conception of his real vocation or his happiness therein. The point is that no extraneous activity, secular in character, may so absorb the heart and mind of a priest that he becomes estranged from the ideals of his true calling. In all situations and in all circumstances the pulse beat of his heart, the disposition of his soul, the core of his personality, and the whole trend of his life must remain priestly. Then no danger will threaten his priestly vocation with profanation, or menace the happiness of his priestly heart.

Hence not every priest is obliged to be a pastor of souls in the strict sense of the word, although there can be no doubt that this form of sacerdotal activity corresponds most perfectly to the essence and purpose of the priesthood. Today as in the past, many priests are engaged in labors that are only loosely connected with the specific tasks of the ministry. Nevertheless they are genuine priests in the full meaning of the words and they often accomplish more for the honor of God and the salvation of mankind than those actually engaged in the cure of souls. The field in which a priest can be active outside the specifically sacerdotal sphere is practically limitless; after all, there is no reputable labor or activity which could not be taken over by the priest. As examples of this in our own time, we point to the former director of the papal observatory in the Roman College, Father Angelo Secchi (d. 1878), and to the late Austrian Chancellor and eminent statesman, Monsignor Ignaz Seipel (d. 1932). Both were men whose fields of labor lay far outside the specific duties of priestly vocation, but they remained priestly to the depths of their souls: their entire extra-sacerdotal activity was animated by the priestly spirit. Such outstanding priestly figures are most useful and beneficial to science and Christianity, to Church and state alike.

Priests of this type do not contradict in the slightest the fundamental requirement, set down above, that the priest must always and in first place be nothing else but a priest, and that the bond between priesthood and priest may never be broken or even weakened.

3. In view of this close and morally indissoluble link between office and incumbent where priestly vocation is concerned, the grave question arises: What benefit does the priest derive from his priesthood? Or, to phrase it differently: What does this vocation, to which he is wedded for life, offer him? Or, to put the question in still another form: What are the joys and blessings, what is the natural and the supernatural happiness of a priestly life? And a second question also clamors for an answer: Does not the priesthood contain exceptional hazards and special dangers to salvation, which in certain circumstances might become disastrous to the individual priest? Both questions must be dealt with as completely as possible, since the seminarian who intends to dedicate his whole person for life to the priesthood has the right to receive full and frank information on these decisive points. In both instances they are questions that must be answered from the viewpoint of eternity and the supernatural, since they have to do not with external and secondary things, but with matters of

vital importance, that affect the individual's happiness in this life and particularly in the life to come. It is not unreasonable when a seminarian, standing before the gates of the sanctuary, thinks of his own soul and its eternal salvation, and before his own conscience asks himself the question: How will my personal and eternal salvation be assured and promoted in this vocation? Against what special difficulties and dangers to my eternal welfare must I be on my guard from the very outset?

2. THE PRIESTHOOD AS A SOURCE OF BLESSING TO THE PRIEST

1. The priesthood is rightly called a difficult and exacting vocation which burdens a man with extraordinary responsibility before God and for eternity. St. John Chrysostom called it an office that was too onerous even for the shoulders of angels.[2] On the other hand, we must not forget that precisely this vocation opens up to its members fonts of the richest blessings and reservoirs of the most powerful help. The genuine priest has no reason to tremble and be afraid, as if he were standing alone in his gravely responsible office, as if he were depending exclusively upon his own feeble human power. He is ever under the protection of God and assisted by the strength of God. As a priest he is overshadowed by the power of the Most High, which uses him as a living instrument.

While it is true that the servant of God is dependent upon the assistance of grace from above in all his priestly functions and in his entire priestly life, it is likewise true that this assistance is always at his command, and in richest

[2] *De sacerd.*, 1, 3, cap. 4 (*PG*, XLVIII, 642 f.).

abundance. In the first place, of course, this divine support is given him for the sake of others, that he may guide the streams of grace to the souls of men; but in the second place, it is given to him personally, for his own purification, strengthening, and sanctification. In ordination the priest receives the Holy Ghost in a special manner. *Accipe Spiritum Sanctum,* says the ordaining bishop in the name of God and of the Church. This conferring of the Holy Spirit is not a mystical fiction without meaning or content, or an empty symbolical rite; it contains complete truth and reality.

2. And something else must be considered. The sacrament of holy orders not only effects a direct and physical strengthening of the priest by the grace it imparts; it also fortifies him in a more general and moral respect. The fact that he is consecrated, the consciousness of ordination and of the divine mission attached to it, give every priest a unique power and confidence. The realization that he is ordained prevents the priest from ever forgetting he is consecrated to the Lord, that is, that he has been lifted out of the generality of men and placed at the side of God, that through the imposition of hands by the bishop a share of the divine powers has been conferred upon him, powers possessed by men in no other state of life. The recognition of the fact that he has been singled out by God from among thousands and destined for heavenly tasks, that he carries in his hands higher, spiritual, supernatural powers, is for every priest a potent source of protection and strength in his vocational life. The firm conviction that he has been sent and equipped by God differentiates the Catholic priest, intrinsically and essentially, from all others whose life work has to do with the guidance of men and

nations. "For these [i. e., other leaders] believe they have been called to leadership by some subjective aptitude of soul, innate or acquired; that is, by virtue of the special knowledge and the strong will power which they feel they possess." [3]

The priest's consciousness of his consecration and mission is something altogether different from the subjective conviction that a man may have of his own ability to lead others. The priest's conviction is based on a firm belief that he has been called and qualified by God. This conviction lives on in every priest; it is almost as ineradicable as the *character indelibilis* which holy orders has imprinted upon his soul. Lippert makes the following weighty and well-founded observations: "Even in a priest who has fallen grievously and been guilty of serious moral lapses, even in a renegade priest who has sinned against the duty of obedience to his ecclesiastical superiors and perhaps cut himself off entirely from the Church, even in a priest who has lost the faith, the consciousness that he is still a priest is not rooted out; he continues to feel that, by virtue of a special calling vouchsafed to him, he carries in his hands enormous powers and prerogatives. Hence he hardly ever loses the secret yearning for the sublime service of the altar, for the celebration of mass and the reception of the Eucharist. Even when he rejects all other dogmas, he retains the curiously inconsistent inclination to believe in the Blessed Sacrament, aye, even to confect and to receive this sacrament. If such an unfortunate priest ever finds his way back to his pristine vocation and mission, the return in most cases is traceable to the desire to be allowed once more

[3] Lippert, *Vom guten Menschen* (1931), p. 233.

to live and labor as a dispenser of the mysteries of God." [4]

3. Further, the divinely called priest is conscious of the close and living relationship existing between himself and Christ; he is in intimate spiritual union with the eternal High Priest whose work it is his mission to continue. We know how strongly the Apostle St. Paul felt himself to be one with Christ; he even dared identify himself personally with our Lord: "And I live, now not I; but Christ liveth in me." [5] From this conviction he drew the almost superhuman confidence and power which never forsook him even in the darkest hours and the most trying situations of his Apostolic ministry: "I can do all things in him who strengtheneth me." [6]

Just as the confidence in God and our Lord, which St. Paul never lost, was based on his selection and calling by God, just as the consciousness and firm belief that he had been *vocatus apostolus* gave St. Paul at all times an unshakable courage, a powerful stimulus, and an Apostolic candor in speech and action, so in like manner the moral power and authority of the priesthood and of the individual priest rest upon the conviction of a divine vocation and a divine mission which receive their indelible seal in the sacrament of holy orders.

The separate orders which the candidate for the sacerdotal state receives, culminating in the order of priesthood itself, impose fresh duties and additional sacrifices upon him, and impart a dignity and a fulness of power that reaches up to heaven. But they do more than this;

[4] *Loc. cit.*, p. 232.
[5] Gal. 2: 20.
[6] Phil. 4: 13.

they confer upon the individual incumbent of this lofty and onerous office the necessary sacramental graces. This means that they give the priest a right to the special assistance of God in all his priestly functions and, beyond that, in his entire priestly and vocational life. The indelible sacerdotal character, impressed upon his soul, enables him to perform his priestly functions in a valid and licit manner; the rich and continuous flow of sacramental grace helps him to discharge these same duties with the required moral worthiness, and to lead a life in conformity with the priestly ideal. The special supernatural assistance of grace, guaranteed the priest by holy orders, corresponds to his special and mounting duties, and endows him with a spiritual power of accomplishment far surpassing his natural ability.

4. In truth, the loyal priest lives in a world that is wholly supernatural, a world of grace, and he daily receives an increase of grace. He lives and breathes in the immediate presence of God. "A deep peace pervades his heart; the judgment of the world, the praise of the world, the contempt of the world, the hatred of the world, no longer affect his heart; for it is at rest in God; in Him and with Him it is elevated high above the world." [7] In this fact of being hidden and secure in God, the priest finds an invaluable source of grace, peace, and holy joy.

Exceptionally rich as a source of grace to the priest is the altar where he daily offers the sacrifice of the New Law. Theologians discuss the manner in which the fruits of grace flowing from every mass are divided among the various participants. The celebrating priest, of course, al-

[7] Hettinger, *Timotheus* (1909), p. 52.

ways has first place among those who derive benefit and grace from the mass. Nor could it be otherwise, since he plays the most important rôle in the celebration of the holy sacrifice. By means of every holy mass which he offers he performs a good action that produces supernatural merit *ex opere operantis,* according to his personal worthiness and devotion. This merit is greater than the merit gained by other pious works, such as fasting and similar acts of penance, which cannot be compared with the holy sacrifice of the mass in objective worth. The degree of this merit obviously depends upon the priest's dispositions and co-operation. The better his remote and immediate preparation, the greater his devotion and attention during mass, and the purer the intention with which he performs this sacrificial action, the richer will be the merit and the increase of grace that come to him *ex opere operantis.*

When we think of the grace that the mass produces *ex opere operato,* we realize that the priest who says mass worthily is not left empty-handed. Theologians teach that each mass produces a threefold fruit: (*a*) *fructus generalis,* which goes to all those present, then to the pope, the diocesan bishop, and the Church as a whole; (*b*) *fructus specialis,* the disposal of which depends on the celebrant's personal intention; and (*c*) *fructus specialissimus,* which is destined for the celebrating priest personally. In conformity with the character of holy mass itself, this very special fruit can take effect in the form of petition, reparation, or satisfaction—all to the advantage of the priest himself, and indeed in such a way that he cannot waive his claim to this fruit or its effects in favor of someone else.[8] And so the

8 Cf. Pohle-Preuss, *The Sacraments,* II, 390 ff.

worthy priest experiences each morning at the altar not only an edification and exaltation of spirit, but also a decided enrichment and strengthening of his soul in grace.

5. Something similar is true of the priest's other sacred functions, whether there is question of sacrament or sacramental. These holy rites can and should be meritorious works for the priest, bringing him grace and eternal reward. In their administration he guides the streams of God's grace to the souls of others, and his own soul also imbibes at the fountains of salvation. Here too, all depends on the personal worthiness and the good intention of the ministering priest.

When we reflect upon all these things, we readily see that it is no exaggeration to assert that the priest is surrounded by a peculiarly rich spiritual world, that he lives and breathes in an atmosphere saturated with the grace of God.

But what if the priest, in spite of these enormous spiritual advantages, deviates from the path of virtue and becomes a victim of sin? In such a sad event, which unfortunately happens from time to time, the fault certainly is not with priestly vocation or the grace of God; it lies solely in the misuse of the erring priest's free will. Even when surrounded by a sea of divine grace, the will retains its freedom, a freedom that can decide for good or evil. God's grace never coerces the will of man.

6. Prayer is another support of the priest and a font of grace for his soul. The Church obligates him to the daily recitation of the breviary, called in liturgical language the *officium divinum;* she also admonishes him earnestly to make a daily meditation, and exhorts him in general to

the practice of a fervent devotional life. In short, the priest is expected to be a man of prayer. By the many prayers which should accompany and fructify his day's work, he surrounds his soul with an invigorating supernatural atmosphere and equips himself with spiritual strength. This is particularly true of the breviary which the priest recites in the name of the Church and at her command. He must exercise great care, therefore, lest he regard this form of liturgical prayer merely as a duty imposed by Church law and think of it only under the ominous name, *onus diei;* it should rather be considered as a powerful aid to piety and personal sanctification.[9]

7. Finally, the ministry itself, the office of good shepherd and of spiritual father to his congregation, furnishes the priest with another valuable aid in his spiritual life, and opens up fresh sources of grace to his soul. Many a priest at work in the pastoral field will no doubt feel inclined to contest this statement, pointing to the countless vexations and hardships, the many disappointments and apparently futile labors and sacrifices, that the present-day ministry entails. It is true that the priest is often assigned to a portion of the vineyard which is far from promising; the hard and stony soil can be cultivated only at the cost of arduous labor. But even such a state of affairs does not militate against the truth of the statement set down at the beginning of this paragraph. Viewed supernaturally, even the most difficult cure of souls contains much that enriches the priest spiritually, and many things that bring him heartfelt consolation and quiet priestly joy.

[9] Cf. Stockums, "Das Brevier im religiös-aszetischen Leben des Priesters" in *Zeitschrift für Theologie und Seelsorge* (1929), pp. 323–39.

In this case, too, everything depends on the focus of the priest's attention and on his viewpoint regarding his pastoral field and his pastoral labor. A priest who is concerned primarily about external success and tangible results will in most cases be bitterly disappointed, as also will the one who counts on the recognition and gratitude of men. But the priest who from the start has a spirit of humble and unselfish devotion, the priest who brings with him a supernatural readiness to make sacrifices, will not easily be discouraged, much less embittered in his heart, by disappointments and apparent lack of success. The priest who is a good shepherd after the model of his Master is gifted with the proper perspective; he does not always view things pessimistically and in a spirit of faultfinding; he does not see merely the evil in the world and in man. Such a priest exercises his ministry with invincible love and patience, and discovers even on hard and stony ground many a flower that delights his heart. It all depends on the ability to see such hidden beauties. Many times the situation resembles that of two travelers who are journeying together through barren country; the one sees on every side hidden mysteries and beauties of nature that delight his eye, while the other sees nothing but dreary stretches of wasteland.

Consoling experiences and quiet priestly joys are part of the ministry even in the stoniest and thorniest pastoral field. The clear eyes of little children who look up to the priest in all innocence and purity, the repentance of a contrite sinner who with the help of the priest has been reconciled to God, the wrestling of this or that soul for purity and virtue in a struggle that is known to the priest alone, the lilylike beauty of an unsullied heart—all these are priestly joys found on every side, even where at a superficial glance one would least expect them, namely, in the most abandoned quarters of our large cities. Considered from a human standpoint, such joys constitute a full compensation for the various unpleasant and discouraging concomitants of pastoral work in a great metropolis.

Up to this point we have said nothing of the superabundant opportunities for the practice of charity that the pastoral office affords. The commandment to love our neighbor is second only to the command to love God. The pastoral office rightly deserves to be called the school of Christian charity and mercy. Just as all the labors of a pastor of souls, viewed in the light of supernature, are meritorious acts for himself, so they are without exception acts of Christian charity—spiritual and, in many cases, also corporal acts of mercy. All priestly activity, specifically the care of souls, can without more ado be regarded and appraised as an unbroken work of charity and as the loftiest service of mankind. That the exercise of charity in general and of pastoral charity in particular prepares an overflowing measure of sublime satisfaction will be denied by no one who understands and feels what it means to give help to others. The consciousness of having performed a good deed and of having assisted others is in itself a sufficient reward, prescinding from the supernatural reward that will come from God and that has been promised even for the drink of water given in His name. The priest in the active ministry must have a heart and an understanding for this phase of his vocation; he must never allow vexation and resentment to rob him of the

gold of benevolence placed in his soul by God at the time
of his calling to the priesthood. The love and kindliness
of a genuine priestly heart have always proven stronger
than all the stubbornness and wickedness of men. A
sublime example of this was furnished by the saintly Curé
of Ars; assigned to an utterly ruined parish, he succeeded
in gradually conquering the most obdurate hearts by his
boundless love and patience.

8. Negatively also the priesthood is a source of blessing
to the priest. Like a protecting wall, it guards his soul from
many snares and temptations that menace secular callings.
The concupiscence of the flesh and of the eyes, the world
with its manifold perversity and malice, must halt before
the gates of a priesthood that is preserved untarnished. Not
as if the priest, by the very fact that he has been anointed
with holy chrism, ceases to be a man of flesh and blood,
a man with all the weaknesses of human nature. He remains that even after ordination. But the priesthood with
its renunciation of the world and of self, practiced out of
love for God and souls, the priesthood with its detachment
from purely earthly and profane interests, acts like a strong
wall of defense, holding at a distance all injurious and
ruinous influences. Just as the clerical garb of a priest is
an outward sign of his dignity and also a protection that
should not be underestimated, so the priesthood itself is a
far-reaching safeguard to the individual priest because of
the atmosphere with which it surrounds him. As long as
the priest living in the midst of the world remains spiritual
and true to the ideals of his vocation, as long as he keeps
the priestly motto, "Holy to the Lord," [10] ever before his

[10] Ex. 28: 36.

eyes, then he is, as it were, surrounded by impregnable walls shielding him from hostile assaults. Within these walls he enjoys security and seclusion; he lives in a happy world of blessing and grace, a world known only to himself and unknown to the man of the world.

9. But the question immediately arises whether this seclusion, these invisible walls within which the priest is enclosed, do not deprive him of the full joy of living. Is not such an existence a sad and joyless thing? In the eyes of a passionate man of the world such would indeed be the fact, but actually it is not so. Pure and noble joy is not joined so closely and so abundantly with any other calling as with genuine, unsullied priestly vocation.

As a matter of historical fact, the reproach that it was a religion of joylessness and world weariness was leveled at Christianity from the very beginning. And yet, no other religion has so staunchly championed real joy, both in its justification and in its realization, as Catholic Christianity has. There is no need for proof to establish this often distorted fact; at any rate, it lies beyond the scope of our task. We content ourselves with pointing out briefly that Christianity at its first coming into the world was expressly characterized as the gospel of joy: "For behold, I bring you good tidings of great joy, that shall be to all the people." [11]

Repeatedly and in an impressive manner, our Lord Himself promised the Apostles, in addition to a unique peace of heart, an overflowing joy, a joy far superior to the fleeting joys of this world, a joy that would be their permanent possession: "Your joy no man shall take from you." [12]

[11] Luke 2: 10.
[12] John 16: 22.

This joy, designed in the first place for the disciples, would not be taken from their hearts by persecution and suffering; rather, and herein lies another Christian paradox, it would gain fresh impetus from such cruel visitations and reach its full flowering, so that all sadness would be dissipated: "Blessed are ye when they shall revile you, and persecute you, and speak all that is evil against you, untruly, for my sake: be glad and rejoice, for your reward is very great in heaven." [13] No one was more saturated with this fundamental Christian conception which countenances no sorrowful pessimism than St. Paul, whose heart was full of joy in sad days as well as in happy days: "I exceedingly abound with joy in all our tribulation." [14] It was no empty phrase or a form of autosuggestion, but an honest and personally experienced conviction that found expression in his admonition to the new Christians: "Rejoice in the Lord always." [15]

How could the priesthood, the loftiest state within the Christian dispensation, fail to participate in this Christian joy? The priest is called and privileged to share in the vicissitudes and sufferings of Christ and His Church; but he also has a special right to drink at the fountains of joy and blessing that are accessible only to the priesthood.

We pointed out above that even the priest who is sent to a seemingly stony portion of the vineyard enjoys a multitude of quiet, interior joys, which only a priestly heart has the faculty to feel and appreciate. Wherein, ultimately, lies the deep source of all this consolation and happiness

[13] Matt. 5: 11 f.
[14] See II Cor. 7: 4.
[15] Phil. 4: 4.

that come to the divinely called priest? Nowhere else than in priestly vocation itself and in the glad consciousness that he is a priest. All the spiritual power of the Catholic priest is based, in the last analysis, on this conviction of his divine selection and priestly mission; and also all the joys that come to him, joy in privation and sacrifice, and, if need be, holy joy in martyrdom, emanate from the same source.[16] Unlike many others, the priest does not seek to find joy and consolation for his soul outside his vocation, but exclusively in his holy vocation itself. "For he carries God in his heart, and in Him he finds an inexhaustible font of joy." [17]

10. Lastly, we must not overlook the priest's hopes and expectations for eternity. Consoling beyond description is the death of a good priest. *Sub specie aeternitatis* he, as a youth, once made the decision to serve God in the priesthood. In the light of eternity and for eternity he exerted himself and spent himself in the ministry; as pastor of souls, he perhaps was instrumental in leading many from error to truth, and in preparing a great number of souls for a happy eternity. Loyal to his vocation, he conscientiously preached the eternal truths; full of renunciation and self-denial, but also of holy joy, he walked in the ways of God, never permitting himself to be misled by the shams and deceptions of a seductive world. He was a man of God through and through, a man who sought no worldly honors, a man who despised fame, perishable gain, and the foolish praise of men. He preferred to remain hidden from the world with Christ, and to live only for God. The prom-

---

[16] Lippert, *Vom guten Menschen* (1931), p. 234; also pp. 227–45.
[17] Hettinger, *Timotheus* (1909), p. 53.

ise of God to Abraham shone with heavenly brightness before his eyes: "I am thy protector, and thy reward exceeding great."[18] As a devout priest, he had the right to apply this promise to himself.

And now he stands before the portals of eternity. Perhaps he is a venerable old man, grown gray in the service of the Lord, or perhaps he is a man, young in years, who has used up his vital energy in laborious toil in the Lord's vineyard. Bidding goodbye to life and labor, he may say with St. Paul in happy hope and complete confidence: "I have fought a good fight, I have finished my course, I have kept the faith. As to the rest, there is laid up for me a crown of justice, which the Lord the just judge will render to me in that day."[19]

In view of the accounting that he must give to the eternal and just Judge, he naturally feels oppressed with a sense of heavy responsibility. And that is altogether comprehensible. Much was entrusted to him by God; much also will be expected of him. But need he tremble and be afraid for that reason? He had his failings and weaknesses; he has sinned, perhaps even grievously, but he has also confessed his guilt with heartfelt contrition and deep humility; he never fell a victim to a proud and self-righteous disposition. And now the moment has come when he must appear before God, to whose altar he so often ascended during life. God is holy and just, the stern judge of all evil. During his priestly life, the dying priest had often preached to this effect in words of warning and admonition to the faith-

[18] Gen. 15: 1.
[19] See II Tim. 4: 7 f.

ful. But God is also a merciful father, a God full of forgiving gentleness, a God whose most beautiful and divine attribute is His infinite mercy.

Not relying on his own merits but with firm confidence in God's mercy, the priest may with happy heart undertake the journey to eternity. He will not be cast aside and condemned, but will be received as a good and faithful servant, clasped in God's embrace, and told to enter into the joy of his Lord. Even though heaven should not open to him immediately, even though he must still undergo a process of purification, he is sure of eternal salvation, of heaven; the beatific vision with its never ending happiness is no longer in danger of being lost. He carries this consoling consciousness with him to purgatory.

The heaven of the priest has its own beauties. The soul of the saved priest shines with the splendor of the indelible character, the divine seal of his priesthood, impressed upon it on the day of ordination. His head bears the crown of virginity and the glory of the stars promised by God to those who have instructed many unto justice.[20] Now he sees the Son of God in His heavenly transfiguration and glory, the same divine Son for whom he so often prepared a sacramental existence on earth; he sees the Holy Ghost as the personified love of the Father and the Son, the same Holy Spirit whom he so often served as an instrument of grace in the days of his earthly ministry. In blessed love and gratitude he sinks to his knees with the angels and saints before the throne of the All-highest to join in the eternal *Sanctus,* the same greeting with which while on

[20] Cf. Dan. 12: 3.

earth he so often saluted his God during the holy sacrifice of the mass.

The Apostle St. Paul assured the early Christians: "When Christ, our life, appears, you also will appear with him in glory." [21] Is not the hope proper and justified that the loyal priest, who was another Christ on earth, will appear in the first ranks of those at the side of the glorified Christ on that day when the Lord will return with great power and majesty to judge the living and the dead? "When Christ appears, then he also will appear; Christ's glory will then cast its reflection over him." [22]

Who knows? Perhaps here on earth the priest was unknown to the world, but he was known to God by his virtues, and that is sufficient. On earth the priest may have had the same experience as St. Paul, who was treated as the refuse of this world; [23] he was perhaps made a spectacle to the world, but in the eyes of God he was a jewel, and now this jewel sparkles for all eternity.

3. SPECIAL DANGERS TO SALVATION IN THE PRIESTHOOD

1. To treat the subject of the priesthood and the priest by showing only the bright side and ignoring the dark side of the picture would be obviously unfair. A just, objective judgment requires that both, the somber as well as the sunny side, be considered. Consequently we must now call attention to the unique difficulties and hardships, to the pitfalls

---

[21] Col. 3: 4.
[22] Hettinger, *loc. cit.*
[23] Cf. I Cor. 4: 9.

and dangers to salvation, that lie in priestly vocation. By virtue of his office the priest lives in a special world of grace, but also in a special world of danger. In an earlier chapter we emphasized that it would be a narrow, even inadequate, motive for priestly vocation, if the candidate were to enter the sacerdotal state with the sole intention of thereby saving his own soul; we stressed the truth that the primary purpose and goal of this state of life are to mediate grace and salvation to others. A priest, therefore would have a fundamentally incorrect conception of his vocation, if he were to console himself with the thought that he is sure to be saved simply because he is a priest, as though the priesthood in itself were an absolutely certain guaranty of eternal salvation.

The priesthood is nothing of the sort. Such an idea, especially if entertained by the the priest himself or by the one who intends to become a priest, might easily lead to disastrous disillusionment. In regard to the individual's own salvation, every state of life has its own helps and advantages, and also its own obstacles and dangers. The priesthood, in spite of the tendency of many to see in it only the advantages, is no exception to the general rule. No priest or seminarian must imagine that all dangers to his own soul and his own personal salvation are a priori excluded in this vocation.

An earnest consideration of this truth should not frighten divinely called candidates who are striving after an ideal, or dissuade them from taking the road that leads to the priesthood. Such reflections should rather spur them on to a searching examination of conscience and a thorough testing of themselves, before they undertake the decisive step. Above all, such thoughts should serve to bring the unfit and uncalled candidate to his senses, so that, before it is too late for him to retrace his steps, he will give up the intention of becoming a priest.[24]

2. The fact that the priestly state contains hazards to salvation is conclusively proved by experience and history. No one can deny, and no one should forget, that the story of the Catholic priesthood as a whole, from the days of Christ to our own, presents a glorious picture, unrivaled by any other vocation in life. No other state has even approached the priesthood in the number of its outstanding personalities; no other state of life has produced so many great saints as the priesthood and the episcopacy.

On the other hand, we must also admit that in every age individual members of the clergy have themselves erred and suffered shipwreck, and have also carried many others with them to destruction. We are not able, in fact we have no right, to pronounce with absolute certainty a sentence of eternal damnation *in concreto* over any person, priest or layman, who has turned away from God and remained impenitent to the very end of his life. God alone is the one who can pronounce the judgment that determines the eternal fate of an individual, and His mercy is unfathomable and infinite. His grace is able to save the hardened sinner even in the last instant of his life. Hence the Church, even when she has been forced to exclude a sinner from her communion on earth, has never considered herself authorized to speak over

---

[24] Cf. Lohmann, *Über den Priesterstand* (1899), pp. 168–201; Dieckhoff, *Über den Beruf und die Vorbereitung zum geistlichen Stande* (1859), pp. 35–66. The remarks of the former regarding the dangers of daily holy communion must of course be modified in certain essential points to be brought into agreement with the decree of Pius X on First Holy Communion.

him a sentence of condemnation that would have validity
for eternity. Not even the unfortunate Apostle Judas is an
exception. The Church's judgment in such a case is always
conditional: the sinner is lost eternally, only if he does not
repent. On the other hand, the Church has the courage to
make positive judgments in the opposite direction and to declare that many of her members, whom she identifies by
name and station, have entered into eternal bliss and are to
be venerated as blessed and holy.

But in spite of the fact that we on earth have no right to
pass a premature judgment or to anticipate in the slightest the
justice of God, we still recognize that the death of many
a person occurs under such unfavorable conditions that, humanly speaking, we have grave reason to fear the worst for
the eternity of many a sinner. And in that unhappy class is
found more than one priest.

The history of the heresies and schisms that have afflicted
the Church tells a sad story. Almost invariably and with few
exceptions, consecrated priests have been to blame for the
devastating defections and divisions that have inflicted so
many grievous wounds upon the mystical body of Christ
in the course of the centuries. This was true of Arius in the
ancient Church, it was true of Luther in the sixteenth century, and it is true of the heretics of more recent times. Entire
nations and peoples were robbed of their faith or cut off from
the center of Christian unity through the fault of priests.
What a responsibility to shoulder before the judgment seat
of God, what a burden to carry along into eternity! And
priests are the ones who have dared to do just this. We are
reminded of the terrible words of our Lord: "Woe to the
world because of scandals. For it must needs be that scandals

come: but nevertheless woe to that man by whom the scandal cometh." [25] Very rarely has a priestly heretic or schismatic found his way back to the Church and repented before his death; by far the greater number have remained blind and obdurate to the very end of their lives. Their fate in eternity, prescinding from a miracle of divine grace in the last instant, can hardly be in doubt.

Church history further speaks of periods of moral decay among nations. We need think only of the time when the abuses in the matter of benefices were at their worst, or of the time immediately preceding the Protestant Revolt. To the shame of the clergy it must be said that representatives of the priestly state—bishops, priests, and religious who had fallen a prey to worldliness and immorality—were the ones who gave impetus to the growing demoralization and decadence of the people. Like shepherd, like flock. Since many shepherds in those dark days forgot the dignity and purpose of their mission and gave themselves over to loose living, it was inevitable that the flock also should decline in discipline and morality, appealing to the conduct of the shepherds as an excuse, perhaps even as a justification, for its own immorality.

Melancholy happenings in the recent past and in the immediate present are still too fresh in our memory to require mention here. Unhappy priests, hardened in sin, are living in the world today, and we can think of their last hour and their future lot in eternity only with fear and trembling. Like the recantation of the heretic or the schismatic, the conversion of the priest who has suffered moral shipwreck is extremely difficult and extremely rare. In many cases where the erring layman raises himself up and returns home to

[25] Matt. 18: 7.

God, the erring priest remains obdurate and unresponsive
to God's grace. Scandal and apostasy, blindness and contu-
macy, at times even fanatical hatred of the Church—it is
indeed terrible even to think of the ending to such a priestly
life.

And so, history and experience prove that the priesthood
is by no means an absolute guaranty of salvation for the
individual priest. Even if an unfortunate priestly life does not
always end as disastrously and in such manifest ruin as we
have just described, even if many a priestly tragedy is enacted
in secret, without coming to public knowledge and without
causing much scandal, these circumstances do not remove
the anxious fear that there are priests who are eternally lost,
and that there will be priests in the future to suffer the same
fate.

Confronted with this alarming situation, we are at once
prompted to inquire concerning the special dangers that
flow specifically from the priestly state and that are connected
with the unique nature of this office. Such an inquiry will
point out the possible sources of danger and emphasize the
need of caution and prudence. We intend, therefore, to
consider briefly, not all, but only the most important and the
most common of these dangers.

3. The first specific danger to a priest's salvation lies in the
absolute irrevocability attached to his state of life. Above the
entrance to the sanctuary is chiseled the inscription: *Nun-
quam retrorsum*. Before God and conscience no retreat is
possible, once the threshold of the sanctuary has been crossed
and the oil of ordination applied. The priest remains bound
to his holy vocation forever and always. Strictly speaking,
the Church could indeed loose the priestly ties, specifically

the obligation of celibacy which she has imposed upon the priest, but as a matter of fact and for the weightiest and most prudent reasons she never does so. She never dispenses the unfaithful priest from celibacy, not even when the ex-priest has been juridically demoted to the ranks of the laity.

Because of the indissoluble character of the heavy obligations the candidate for the subdiaconate is about to assume, he is solemnly and earnestly called upon by the bishop to weigh the grave responsibility that confronts him: "But if you receive this order, you will no longer be at liberty to recede from your resolution, but you will be obliged to serve God perpetually (to serve whom is to reign); and with His assistance to observe chastity." [26]

From a human and psychological standpoint, this yoke which he cannot shake off and this obligation which is his for life can beget grave dangers for the soul and the eternal salvation of the individual priest. *Per se* it is not something unusual or incomprehensible if a person in the course of the years changes his views, his inclinations, and his decisions, so that in mature life he thinks differently about many things than he did in the days of his youth. His own internal development, as well as the influences of the world about him, sometimes alter his character and his whole outlook on life. Former ideals that drew his heart with irresistible power lose their attraction and at times vanish altogether. He acquires new perspectives; new aims captivate his soul. Because of these and other influences the individual's relation to his vocation is thrown out of joint. The calling that he had once embraced with real inclination no longer satisfies his heart, and he gradually loses all active interest in it.

[26] *Pontificale Romanum, de ordine subdiaconi.*

Such transformations and changes can occur in all vocations, in the case of laymen as well as of priests. They often mark the beginning of a tragedy in a person's life, unless he is able, even in later years, to undertake a change of vocation or at least to find some other soul-satisfying activity in addition to the purely external practice of the vocation he has come to dislike. In the circumstances the layman can help himself in this manner.

But such a way out is altogether closed to the priest. If lasting dislike and dissatisfaction with regard to his vocation set in, what can he do? He cannot change his vocation. It is indeed possible to change the place and the specific nature of his priestly activity, and in many instances such a change of scene or of labor often succeeds in saving the situation. But he remains a priest, no matter where he is and no matter what special priestly activity he wishes to indulge in. If his dissatisfaction has to do with the essence of his vocation and his priestly duties, then no one can free him from the burden; he remains bound for his entire life. This circumstance is calculated only to heighten the internal dissatisfaction of the unfortunate priest; it may so aggravate the distemper of his soul that his lot becomes simply unbearable, unless he succeeds somehow in coping with it by natural and supernatural means.

Another solution, to which the layman may turn as a last resort, is also denied to the priest. The latter, when his heart is no longer in his work, cannot adapt himself to the unchanging character of his vocation by trying to fulfil his duties in a purely mechanical manner, and then look for personal and interior satisfaction somewhere else. And why cannot the priest do this? Because the priestly office demands of its incumbents their whole soul and their whole personality; it will not tolerate divided allegiance. Unlike the layman, the priest must be heart and soul in his vocation; otherwise he will be an inwardly torn and fundamentally unhappy man.

And what follows? A priest who is at odds with himself and his vocation runs the danger of gradually losing his priestly sense and his priestly spirit, as well as the internal connection between himself and the duties of his calling. He stands at the altar without any fervor, he mounts the pulpit and preaches without any warmth, he sits in the confessional and visits the school without any love or zeal for souls. How can such a priest find words of faith and consolation at the bedside of the sick and dying, how can be perform his priestly prayer, the breviary, with decorum, attention, and devotion? He lacks the priestly heart, and where that is lacking, everything is lacking. In the end he becomes distasteful even to himself; he feels loathing and disgust even for holy things. Wherever he appears as a priest, he feels the weight of the chains pressing down upon him, chains that he cannot throw off without guilt. His life is a living lie, and he groans under the yoke of an internal discord, that he would like with all his strength to cast off, but cannot.

When a priest of God has fallen into so sad and pitiable a state, there is no other help but that he strive earnestly to recapture his former love of vocation and to resurrect his lost ideals. If he wishes to save his soul in eternity, persevering prayer and complete self-conquest are necessary. Frequently the effort is successful, but not always.

4. A second specific danger to salvation, inherent in the priesthood, is the priest's daily and intimate association with holy and divine things. Each day he ascends to the altar, each

day he performs the most sacred action imaginable, each day he receives the bread of angels. Hardly a day passes when he is not called to administer some sacrament or to perform some action that brings blessing to others. *Per se* this continuous association with holy things is for the priest himself a never failing source of good and of spiritual joy.

But not necessarily so. *Cotidiana vilescunt.* Familiarity breeds contempt. Even the most sublime and holy things that, as a mortal man, the priest approached only with fear and trembling in the beginning of his ministry can, when he handles them daily and when his eyes behold the divine in them only under an earthly veil, sink to the level of the ordinary and the profane. We can make this psychological observation on ourselves with regard to the things we come in daily contact with. What habitually passes through our hands and daily engages our attention loses value and dignity in our eyes, so that we experience a lessening of our love and reverence even for the *sanctum* and the *tremendum.* The priest who does not each day renew his pristine fervor is in real danger of substituting for the recollection and devotion with which he celebrated mass and administered the sacraments in the beginning a stolid indifference and a scandal-giving lukewarmness. He is likely to exercise his high office in the manner of a businesslike functionary, and not like a zealous priest. Inevitably such a priest will make himself guilty of countless sins of negligence and irreverence, and thereby place the salvation of his immortal soul in grave jeopardy.

Every day and every hour of the day the priest must live in the state of grace; more than that, he must be concerned about living in a purer and more spiritual atmosphere, an atmosphere that lifts him high above the ordinary and earthly plane. But to achieve this he must practice incessant self-control and self-sanctification. If he is remiss in applying such means, the continuous association with holy things will breed indifference; only a short step separates indifference from the impairment of his tender love for God and divine things, and even from a weakening of his faith itself.

The man of God can meet this threatening danger in no way except by nourishing his inner life of faith and by cultivating a devout intercourse with his God through the practice of daily prayer and by earnest meditation on the eternal truths. To save his own soul he must make it a matter of conscience to use zealously all the ordinary and extraordinary means for personal sanctification that the Church places at his command. Only then will he be able to keep his way of thought and his way of life on the lofty plane demanded by his vocation. *Nostra autem conversatio in caelis est.*[27]

The conclusion to be drawn from these reflections is obvious. The aspirant to the clerical state has the urgent duty of serious self-examination and of seeking the counsel of experienced priests regarding his vocation. Concern for the salvation of his own soul, for which he alone is chiefly responsible, demands it. What will it profit him if he saves the souls of others and loses his own in the process? He must test himself to determine whether he possesses the necessary spiritual foundations and aptitudes that warrant a close and vocational association with divine and holy things without harm to his own salvation. A presumptuous reliance on the grace of God is out of place. Here as elsewhere the axiom,

[27] Phil. 3: 20.

gratia supponit naturam, holds true. The function of grace is to elevate and perfect nature. When nature itself is deficient, that is, where the natural aptitude and the natural basis are lacking, the grace of God will operate in vain.

5. Just as daily association with holy things has its dangers, so also can the frequent preoccupation with what is unholy and sinful become a source of peril to the soul of the priest. In the life of a priest, especially of a pastor of souls, the confessional holds a place second only to the altar. If the one is a potential source of danger, so is the other. The confessional makes the priest directly acquainted with the manifold sins and weaknesses, the passions and vices, of men. No one gazes so deeply and clearly into the sinful heart of man as the priest does in the confessional where the penitent discloses the most secret recesses of his heart; no one learns to know the satanic power and malice of sin in such concrete form as the confessor, to whom sin-tortured souls flee and reveal secrets that are told to no other person.

In itself, there is no special danger in thus becoming acquainted with sin, more particularly when deep contrition accompanies the confession of them. Such encounters with vice, which reveal the depths to which the sinner has fallen, but also the yearning for God in the heart of a contrite penitent, are rather adapted to fill the priest who in God's stead plays the rôle of the good Samaritan with joy and elation. When he is able to lift up a broken and crushed soul, reconcile it with God, and enable it to share again in the blessings of grace, he experiences a joy found nowhere else.

The confessor gazes with equal joy into totally different hearts, into hearts in which the spotless flower of purity and unsullied innocence is abloom; he comes to know souls that are spending themselves in the service of God and their neighbor, souls that have no desire but to please God by leading holy lives. They are the chosen ones of the Holy Spirit, the souls upon whom He lavishes the hidden but priceless gifts of His divine grace. The priest learns to know them and in all humility to esteem them; he is in a position to derive a holy joy from the sight of such glorious virtue, of such pure and noble striving after perfection.

The profound contrition of the repentant sinner and the unclouded beauty of the stainless soul, that are disclosed to the eyes of the pastor of souls, produce also another good effect. They act as an incentive in his own striving after virtue and holiness. Hence the confessional is a school where the priest can learn valuable lessons for the practice of virtue in his own spiritual life. Viewing the sacrament of penance from this angle, we can easily understand why saintly priests have a special love and enthusiasm for the arduous labor of the confessional. In recent times the glorious example set by the saintly Curé of Ars is a case in point.

In spite of the spiritual benefits which the priest can obtain from the administration of the sacrament of penance, the confessional can nevertheless become for him a special danger to salvation, and it actually does become such a source of danger to every priest who does not exercise this responsible office with the greatest circumspection. The danger threatens as soon as the priest begins to fulfil his duties as confessor carelessly and indifferently; he exposes himself to spiritual harm as soon as his real interest in the confessional begins to wane and as soon as he proceeds to this duty in a merely mechanical and external manner.

Bodily fatigue, arising from long and arduous hours in the

confessional or from the routine nature of so many confessions, may furnish the first occasion for incipient indifference and carelessness. But what incalculable harm to souls will result if this spirit of carelessness is allowed to grow, what harm to the souls of penitent and confessor alike! Heavy, indeed, are the guilt and responsibility which such a lax priest loads upon himself. He is supposed to be a physician, a judge, a counselor, in the place of God. In reality he is none of these things. He becomes rather a destroyer of souls, because of his improper manner of administering the sacrament. Where fatherly instruction and advice are called for, he has nothing to say; where his duty obliges him to show special consideration for the struggling sinner or to temper strictness and severity with kindness, he quietly permits things to go along just as they are. What a crime against his holy office, what a violation of the rights and interests of God, what a calamity for the souls of men, what an injury to himself!

The evil is intensified and becomes more insidious for the priest because in his rôle as confessor he can be supervised and controlled by no one; external incentives and salutary warnings for the conscientious exercise of this office are almost entirely lacking. Since the seal of confession must always remain inviolate, the priest can be summoned before no ecclesiastical tribunal to give an accounting of his activity in the confessional. These special circumstances make the administration of the sacrament of penance extremely dangerous for every priest who does not dedicate himself to this office with the holiest zeal and from the purest spiritual motives.

An added danger, as we have intimated, can arise from the direct and concrete knowledge of sin and vice that comes to the confessor. It is of course true that a profound insight into sin, its hatefulness, and its terrible consequences, has a terrifying and disgusting effect. Alas, it is also true that sins and vices, by the frequency and regularity with which they are confessed and laid bare to the priest, can gradually lose their terrifying aspect. A confessor whose thoughts and desires are not always directed on high may begin to see in the moral aberrations of men something almost matter of course, something almost like a natural necessity, and in the end make nothing of them even as regards his own person. In this way he gradually loses the supernatural detestation of sin, to say nothing of the circumstance that the sin which is told him under the pledge of secrecy may, in its refined malice, perhaps present itself to his imagination as an alluring thing and captivate his senses. Others sin, why not I? This is the seductive question that suggests itself. Instead of putting the dangerous thought aside at once, he toys with it. Sin is knocking at the door of his heart and asking for admittance. The tribunal of penance, that should be a place of grace for his own soul as well as for the souls of others, has through his own fault become for him the way to eternal damnation. In the confessional he has learned to know sin, but he has also forgotten to hate and detest it.

6. A fourth and last danger, specifically connected with the priesthood, must also be mentioned. The sacerdotal virtues of humility and chastity are exposed to unusual temptations and assaults in the life of a priest. Particularly are the life and vocation of a secular priest open to such attacks, whereas the religious enjoys more protection in this respect; the very walls of the cloister shield him from many dangers.

Humility is a fundamental virtue of Christianity in general and of the priesthood in particular. This virtue is based on a just estimation of one's self, and brings man into the proper relationship with God. God is everything; man, in comparison, is nothing. What he is and what he has he owes to God. Without this attitude of humility, there can be no real Christianity and, above all, no real priesthood. Now, what are the special dangers that menace the humility of the priest?

They lie principally in the objective worth and sublimity of the priesthood and in the esteem shown to individual priests by loyal Catholics. It is a foolish and dangerous thing when the priest identifies office and person, and then imagines that all the high regard and veneration which the faithful pay to his office are paid to him personally. Woe to him if he permits himself in this way to acquire a deplorable spirit of conceit and vanity! He will not only lower his own prestige and effectiveness as a priest, but all too easily will shut off the streams of grace so necessary for his own soul. The warning of Holy Writ is meant also for him: "God resisteth the proud, but to the humble he giveth grace." [28]

We need not be surprised if the priest who loses his humility soon succumbs to temptations of ambition and to a craving for power. As we explained in an earlier chapter, the priest, as the servant of Christ and the dispenser of the mysteries of God, has at his command great spiritual power and authority. He looses and binds in the name of God. Men must kneel at his feet and confess their guilt to him as the representative of God. He is empowered, as well as in duty bound, to demand from all, no matter how lofty their rank or station, recognition of his decisions and obedience to his instructions.

Moreover, he exercises great power as a preacher of the

[28] Prov. 3: 34; cf. Jas. 4: 6; I Pet. 5: 5.

word of God, particularly when he has a glowing eloquence at his command. By means of such a talent he is able to hold his audience in his thrall and stir them to the depths of their souls. In truth, the divinely gifted pulpit orator, enlightened by the Holy Spirit, wields an almost uncanny power over the hearts and minds of men. But the priest must realize that this gift of eloquence is not without its element of danger to himself. Recognition and flattering praise from others can spoil him and give him an exaggerated opinion of himself. The immediate and outward success of a sermon, the enthusiasm he arouses, may intoxicate him and go to his head, if he places too much weight on such things. This is the not insignificant danger lurking in the gift of eloquence. If the danger is not perceived and averted in time, the consequences may almost imperceptibly bring about the ruin of a celebrated preacher.

Fortunately such outstanding success in the pulpit is not of frequent occurrence. But every preacher must be on guard against another and more common danger. If he allows himself to form a vain and exaggerated opinion of himself, he will soon lose the real priestly spirit, and preach only himself and human wisdom, instead of Christ crucified.[29] He will then resemble sounding brass and a tinkling cymbal, even though he speaks with the tongue of angels.[30]

7. Next to humility, chastity is a specifically priestly virtue. The priest must be pure of heart. In the continuous exercise of this virtue he must show himself a spiritual man, that is, a man who lives, not according to the lusts of the flesh, but according to the will of the Holy Spirit, a man who is re-

[29] See I Cor. 1: 23.
[30] Ibid., 13: 1.

moved from the sensual and the earthly, a man who breathes
the clean atmosphere of a higher, supernatural world. In
spite of consecration and sacrament he remains a mortal
man; to help him preserve this priestly virtue unspotted, the
Church places at his disposal a variety of spiritual aids, and
cautions him to be sedulous in the use of these means, knowing full well that even men of God carry this precious treasure in earthen vessels.[31]

The sexual instincts are part of human nature and usually
cannot be rooted out by any consecration or grace. According
to the Christian moral law, their gratification must be confined to certain well-defined limits, limits that do not go
beyond the marital union of the sexes. In celibacy, to which
the priest is obligated, the limits are of course drawn much
closer, much narrower, than for the average layman. The
priest is expected to master the strongest sexual urge, both
inwardly and outwardly.

Various dangers to chastity exist for every person of flesh
and blood. Even marriage is not a complete protection. That
the dangers for the priest, particularly for the secular priest,
are much greater than for the average lay person, cannot well
be doubted. As pastor of souls, the secular priest is at the
disposal and command of all, even of the female sex; close
association with women, especially with such as submit themselves to his spiritual guidance or with whom his vocation
brings him in contact in other ways, is practically unavoidable. If in such cases he does not exercise the necessary prudence, if he oversteps the bounds of reserve, then even the
best-intentioned pastoral care of the *genus femininum* and
the apparently harmless association with persons of the op-

[31] See II Cor. 4: 7.

posite sex may become a snare of the devil. Experience speaks a language that cannot be misunderstood.

A special vocational source of danger in regard to chastity lies in the circumstance that the pastor of souls, both in and out of the confessional, is confronted with delicate cases of conscience, which require a detailed mental preoccupation with sexual matters and which must be discussed, no matter how decently. That in such instances he may experience disturbances in his lower nature is not to be wondered at. Such movements in themselves are not sinful, but they easily develop into sin unless they are controlled and kept within bounds. Only the conscientious priest who takes the duty of celibacy seriously and who is concerned about leading an inwardly chaste life will remain unaffected by them and suffer no harm in his inner world of thought and imagination. The priest who conducts himself too freely and imprudently in the circumstances will easily lose his sense of moral delicacy and succumb to the temptations that arise. As a man of strong character, the priest must certainly not be given to an unhealthy prudery or to an exaggerated scrupulosity, but neither may he encourage laxity and perhaps even lasciviousness when treating of moral questions. He should always remember that as a priest he must preserve a priestly tact in all things. If he is faithful in this, he may confidently hope that the grace of his vocation will help and protect him even in the most delicate situations.

With these special dangers to salvation in mind, we can appreciate how outstanding spiritual men like St. John Chrysostom and St. Gregory Nazianzen, to mention only two, strove for a long time and with all their power against assuming the office of priest or bishop. Today also, there is nothing that can so imperil salvation as to enter the priestly state carelessly and without thorough self-examination. Only the man who is prompted by a lofty and pure conception of his vocation furnishes for himself and the Church the necessary guaranty that as a priest he will not harm his own soul and that, with the aid of the sacramental graces that come to him in holy orders, he will successfully meet and overcome all the dangers to salvation, that are connected with the nature and the unique character of the sacerdotal state.

CHAPTER IX

The Personal Sanctification of the Priest

I. THE OBJECTIVE HOLINESS OF THE PRIESTHOOD

1. The priesthood is an objectively holy state, holy in its origin, holy in its nature and goal, holy in its functions. The word "holy" has its own peculiar tone quality that affects particularly the heart and soul. It raises mundane man to a higher world, a world totally different from this visible world of evil and sin, a world that is completely filled with the infinitely holy essence of God. God alone is altogether holy; He is holiness itself. Holy are the immediate surroundings of God in heaven; holy are the angels who cluster about His throne and holy are the souls of the just who have been admitted into His heavenly kingdom.

Holiness was demanded also of the select group of persons who were intimately associated with the Son of God on earth. Holy were the mother and the foster father whom the eternal Father had given Him; by degrees the Apostles whom He Himself had chosen and who were favored with His particular friendship, became holy. The Son of God would not tolerate in His immediate vicinity persons who were not holy or who would not become so.

The same must be true, essentially, of the state of life that still stands in the closest relationship to the Son of God, the state that He uses to perpetuate His life and work on earth. We have seen that the priesthood has no other purpose than to continue the mission of Christ until the end of time, that is, to free men from sin and to sanctify them with the grace of God. Consequently the priesthood *in se* is a holy institution.

The obvious conclusion that must be drawn from these reflections is that the individual members of the priesthood must also be holy. We would be confronted with an inherent and intolerable contradiction if an objectively holy office were to be entrusted to unholy incumbents, and if holy functions were to be performed by unholy ministers. *Sancta sancte!* That which is holy by its very nature and in itself stands in need of holy care and administration, and this necessary requirement in turn presupposes a subjective holiness in those to whom such care and administration are entrusted.

Hence nothing is more clearly expected of those who bear the priestly dignity and power than personal holiness. On the external and on the personal side, the priest is more strictly obligated to the observance of this law than to the fulfilment of any other duty. He must sanctify his own person, and he must strive unceasingly for a steady increase in interior holiness.

2. For wherever the priest acts as a priest and performs priestly functions—whether the celebration of mass, the administration of the sacraments, the preaching of the word of God, or the direction of souls—he finds himself in a sacred atmosphere and comes into direct contact with the holy and the divine. In a previous chapter we spoke of the priest's

power over the *Corpus Christi reale,* a power surpassingly divine and tremendous, and also surpassingly holy, so much so in fact that, strictly speaking, no man would be worthy to exercise it, if God were to demand full parity between the power itself and the one who wields it. When the priest makes use of this power by celebrating the sacrifice of the New Law, thus renewing in an unbloody manner and in the name and person of Christ our Lord's infinitely sublime sacrifice of praise, thanksgiving, petition, and reparation, he moves in an environment where everything is sacred and where he, least of all, may appear as an unholy one. Infinitely holy is the action itself which he as the sacrificing priest performs, and infinitely holy is the Gift which he takes into his consecrated hands. Consecrated or blessed is the house of God, the place where he stands as he performs this action; consecrated and holy is the altar to which he ascends. Consecrated and blessed are the liturgical vestments which he dons and the vessels which he uses; holy are the prayers, the blessings, and the ceremonies that accompany the sacrificial action. In short, altar and sacrifice are fragrant with a superearthly perfume, and everything about them symbolizes what is holy and divine; the mass itself is an action that should have its setting in heaven rather than upon this earth. We are, therefore, indulging in no pious fancy but simply expressing our living faith when we say that the angels of heaven hover about the altar in unseen adoration whenever the priest ascends to the holy place to exercise his august office. Under the appearances of bread and wine, the Son of God is present on the table of sacrifice, having been called down to the altar in His divinity and in His humanity by the words of the priest.

In truth, can we find a holier place on earth than the altar of a Catholic church? Can we even imagine a holier action than the one the priest performs at mass? Whether the mass is celebrated in a majestic cathedral as a solemn pontifical function, adorned with all the riches and beauty of the liturgy, or as a simple low mass in some dark chamber of the Roman catacombs, makes no essential difference. In both cases it is the same infinitely holy sacrifice of the New Covenant.

Now, since everything connected with the mass is surrounded by a holy, super-earthly atmosphere and fragrant with the perfume of heaven, may the priest himself, the performer of this holy action, be the only one participating in it who is not holy? Would not such a state of affairs destroy the homogeneous character and harmony of the whole? For this reason the Church permits no one but a consecrated priest with anointed hands to ascend to the altar of sacrifice. But is even such purely external consecration sufficient? Must not an interior consecration of the person be added to the exterior consecration of the anointing? To ask the question is to answer it in the affirmative. An inwardly unholy priest may not stand in the holy place and perform the holiest action imaginable on earth.

Next to the holy sacrifice are ranged the other sacraments, entrusted to the priest for administration. These potent rites are holy in their origin, since they were directly instituted by Christ as the means by which the graces of His atoning death are applied to the souls of men. Our Lord Himself determined in essence the material and formal constituents necessary for their valid administration. The sacraments are holy also in the rich and significant ritual that accompanies them; the liturgy adorns their administration with a wealth of ceremonies, thus making them rites full of devotional solemnity. The sacraments are holy especially in their effects; they cleanse the soul from guilt of sin and clothe it in the beautiful garment of grace, particularly sanctifying grace which they either impart or, if it is already present, increase in glory and richness.

It is most fitting that these holy means of grace, which are of divine origin and supernatural potency, should be administered only by holy hands. The sacraments are, of course, effective even when imparted by unholy hands. But what harm comes to the one who possesses those unclean hands and who handles holy things unworthily! The unworthy minister indeed mediates God's grace and blessing to others, but himself he drives from sin to sin.

Holy also are the truths and holy are the commandments which the priest proclaims. The word of God, that has come from the All-holy and that possesses eternal truth, is placed on the lips of the priest. His is the lofty duty to announce the same truths that were taught by Christ and the Apostles, truths guarded by the Church from the very beginning as a holy treasure and preserved by her with all the care and reverence she would show for the holy grail. Holy is the moral law that the priest must preach and champion as an expression of the divine will; on its loyal observance depend the salvation and happiness of men. Holy, finally, is the breviary which the priest is bound *sub gravi* to recite every day in the name of the Church, the official prayer that is woven into the woof and warp of priestly life and labor.

Holy truths, holy laws, holy prayers—what do they demand? They demand a holy personality, a man whose life and actions are a faithful mirror of what he preaches to others and of what he demands of others in the name of God; a person who, like Christ, is able to stand before men and say: "Though you will not believe me [i. e., my words], believe the works"; [1] a man whose life is a life of prayer and of holy labor in the spirit of his vocation. And so it must be, so the natural fitness of things requires it. And if it is really so in fact, then blessed and happy is the priest himself, and blessed and fortunate are those to whom this priest has been sent as a pastor of souls.

2. SACRAMENTAL CONSECRATION OF THE PRIEST'S PERSON

1. In the priesthood, consecration of the person is joined to the sublimity of the office. If the unique dignity and objective holiness of the priestly state impose upon the individual member a holy way of life, no less emphatically do the sacramental consecrations imparted to his person make the same demand. Beginning with tonsure and continuing with the four minor and the two major orders, the Church leads the young Levite step by step to the door of the sanctuary, which she opens to him in the order of priesthood.

The priest is a man consecrated to God. *Deo sacer,* is the inscription written on his brow. The ancient Romans had developed the word *sacrum* in their religious thought in order to designate what was cut off from profane use and dedicated inviolate to the gods. Ordinary persons were to treat with holy awe and reverence all things considered *sacra,* whether they were hallowed places and objects, or sacred persons such as the pagan priests and the Vestal virgins.

[1] John 10: 38.

Biblical and ecclesiastical language adopted this classical word and gave it a still deeper meaning. In revealed religion also there are holy places, holy objects, holy actions, and particularly holy persons, men and women consecrated to God; and first among these last is the priest. This was true of the Old Testament; it is also true of the New. Of the priests of Israel we read: "They are consecrated to their God. . . . Let them therefore be holy, because I also am holy." [2] The liturgical fillet encircling the brow of the high priest bore the inscription: "Holy to the Lord," [3] and indicated that the person of the priest possessed a sacred character; but it also reminded the priest himself that he must add an interior and moral holiness to his external consecration.

The priest of the New Law is consecrated to God by means of holy orders, the sacrament of priesthood. This sacred and mysterious initiation, conducted by the Church and distinguishing the priesthood of orders from the general priesthood of the laity, not only impresses the indelible priestly character upon the soul of the priest and enriches him with a wealth of sacramental graces, but effects a holy consecration of his entire person. The entire man is henceforth withdrawn from the realm of the profane and placed at the side of God. He now belongs entirely to God, with all the faculties of his mind, with all the powers of his soul and body; he is dedicated and obligated, inwardly and outwardly, to the service of the Lord.

In this way and no other are we to understand the more profound and mystical meaning of the sacrament of holy orders, the anointing by the bishop, the imposition of hands,

[2] Lev. 21: 7 f.
[3] Ex. 28: 36.

the impressive calling down and conferring of the Holy
Spirit.

2. Consecrated and anointed are the priest's hands that
are destined to bless and sanctify, hands that will touch and
distribute to the faithful the living flesh and blood of the
sacramental Son of God.

Consecrated are the priest's tongue and lips, with which he
is to announce to the people the revelation of God, and join
the angels in their *sanctus,* singing the praises of God. The
lips of the priest are to remind the sinner of the malice and
corruption of sin, but also to bear witness to God's infinite
mercy and boundless goodness; in the sacrament of penance
they are to close the gates of hell and open the doors of
heaven to the contrite; they are to call down God's blessing
upon the living and the dead; finally and most tremendous
of all, they are to call down to the altar the eternal Son of
God Himself.

Consecrated are the eye and sight of the priest. He is en-
abled and privileged to behold in immediate proximity the
holiest of holy things, of course under the veil of earthly appearances. Before his eyes flow the mysterious streams of
grace by means of the visible signs, the holy sacraments. The
priest's eye, enlightened by faith, penetrates through the
outer veils and beholds the holy and the divine, that are hidden from natural sight.

Consecrated are the feet of the priest. Basing his statement
on prophetical words of the Old Testament,[4] St. Paul writes:
"How beautiful are the feet of them that preach the gospel
of peace!"[5] Such are the feet of the priest, which carry him

[4] Is. 52: 7; Nah. 1: 15.
[5] Rom. 10: 15.

up to the mountain of the Lord, the altar, and also to the pulpit where he preaches the glad tidings of peace. His feet carry him to the baptismal font and to the confessional, to hospitals and prisons, to the hovels of poverty and distress, to every place where help and healing, consolation and blessing, are needed.

Consecrated, finally, is the heart of the priest, the living center of his whole personality. The priest's heart, a heart that must burn with love and zeal for God and neighbor and must have enough room to embrace all who are entrusted to his care, must not be touched by sensual love. It must rather resemble an open hearth on which burns an undying fire; the priestly heart must glow with love for God, for Christ, for the Church, and for the immortal souls of men. Large enough to embrace all, the genuine priestly heart beats on the heart of God; it belongs to no man, but to God alone.[6]

When we ponder these things and thus come to realize the close relationship in which the priest, by virtue of his office and consecration, stands to God the source of all holiness, we recognize at once that such a favored person is obligated also to interior and spiritual holiness. What would all anointing and consecration, all the dignity of his station and vocation, avail him, if a corresponding consecration, purity, and holiness of the inner man were not superadded? Only when such an agreement between external consecration and internal holiness is present, do we have a harmonious whole, a complete and happy priest, a priest according to the desire of Christ, a priest according to the heart of God.

But this subjective holiness is demanded not only from reasons of moral congruity, but by considerations for the

[6] Cf. also Hettinger, *Timotheus* (1900), pp. 51 f.

happiness and the eternal salvation of the priest himself. Only a holy priest can be satisfied and happy in his vocation; only such a priest can avoid being crushed by the weight of a body whose individual members have been dedicated to God and the world of supernature. A holy priestly soul will be able to animate the body and its members with priestly strength and enthusiasm; it will give the priest a clear understanding of the meaning and purpose of the external consecration and of the interior holiness that must correspond with it.

3. THE ADMONITIONS OF ST. PAUL

1. The essential purpose of the Christian religion and of the Church culminates in the effort to lead all men along the road of spiritual purification and sanctification to union with God, thereby enabling them to attain their last end in eternity. For that reason no admonition recurs so frequently in Holy Scripture and is so often repeated by the Church as the exhortation addressed to all men that they strive after holiness and perfection. The fundamental law of morality as promulgated by Christ is to the same effect: "Be ye therefore perfect, as also your heavenly Father is perfect," [7] a law which St. Paul expressed when he said: "For this is the will of God, your sanctification." [8]

The will of God in this respect applies to all men who wish to be saved, although it does not apply to all in equal measure and with equal strictness. In the Old Testament and particularly in the New, the members of the priestly state, the servants of the sanctuary, are the ones whom God desires in the

[7] Matt. 5: 48.
[8] See I Thess. 4: 3.

first place to be holy and perfect. With special emphasis Jahve imposed upon the priests of the Old Law the duty of personal sanctification: "For I am the Lord your God: be holy because I am holy." [9]

In the New Law, Christ, the revivifier of the priesthood, demanded a holy life of His Apostles, and also prayed to His heavenly Father for their special sanctification: "Sanctify them in truth." [10]

The Church of succeeding ages has always clearly understood the mind and will of the Master. Of the many witnesses who bear testimony to the fact that striving after personal holiness is a peculiar and essential duty of the priest, we will content ourselves with citing only three: St. Paul, the Church fathers, and the Church herself. Their judgment is authoritative and unanimous.

2. *Ex professo* and at considerable length, St. Paul takes up the question of priestly sanctification in his pastoral epistles to Timothy and Titus. In these letters to the disciples whom he had appointed bishops, his intention was to point out not only how they were to lead to virtue and holiness the faithful entrusted to their care, but also and especially how they were to sanctify themselves. The demands he makes in the latter direction far exceed the average of Christian virtue. The private life of his apostolic disciples, as well as their official and pastoral ministry, was to be permeated through and through with a spirit of unselfishness, motivated by a pure intention, and characterized by continuous striving after personal sanctification. In another place [11] we have studied

[9] Lev. 11: 44.
[10] John 17: 17.
[11] Stockums, *Vocation to the Priesthood* (1937), pp. 188–200.

in detail the moral assumptions and requirements that St. Paul sets down for candidates to the episcopal and priestly office. Here we will merely give the list of virtues which the Apostle drew up for the guidance of his disciples in their personal life and activity; it is a program that has the same validity today as in his time.

The negative virtues which St. Paul is most concerned about and which he urgently recommends to his spiritual sons Timothy and Titus, are unselfishness and flight from worldly mammon. Their lives must be free from ostentation and from all lust for money, even as his was: "But having food, and wherewith to be covered, with these we are content. For they that will become rich, fall into temptation, and into the snare of the devil, and into many unprofitable and hurtful desires, which drown men into destruction and perdition. For the desire of money is the root of all evils; which some coveting have erred from the faith, and have entangled themselves in many sorrows." [12]

This is plain speaking; and experience has amply proved that St. Paul was fully right in thus warning against wealth and the lust for gold. The evidence is overwhelming that Christian virtue, especially priestly virtue, is gravely impaired and gradually dies, if the individual becomes a slave to the lust for money and the spirit of mammon in any form whatever. The secularization of the priest usually begins when he succumbs to a love for what the world prizes most, namely, gold. If this gravest of dangers is not recognized and combated from the start, it will spell the doom of the priestly spirit and of priestly idealism.

St. Paul was fully aware of these dangers that menaced the

[12] See I Tim. 6: 8–10.

new-born priestly office. Hence his earnest warning to Timothy: "But thou, O man of God, fly these things"; to which he adds the positive injunction: "and pursue justice, godliness, faith, charity, patience, mildness. Fight the good fight of faith: lay hold on eternal life, whereunto thou art called, and hast confessed a good confession before many witnesses." [13] To the same effect and almost in the same words, he repeats the warning in his second letter to this disciple: "But flee thou youthful desires, and pursue justice, faith, charity, and peace, with them that call on the Lord out of a pure heart. And avoid foolish and unlearned questions, knowing that they beget strifes. But the servant of the Lord must not wrangle: but be mild towards all men, apt to teach, patient." [14]

In this passage the Apostle lists the most important virtues that ought to adorn the man of God, the priest. In the first place he mentions the theological virtues of faith, hope, and charity, which should keep the priest in closest and most living communion with God and bring his supernatural life to full flower. Then he recommends the most necessary moral virtues. Priest and bishop must practice sincere piety: "Exercise thyself unto godliness. For bodily exercise is profitable to little: but godliness is profitable to all things, having promise of the life that now is, and of that which is to come." [15] Moreover, the priest must be a man of justice and of peace, a man who understands how to deal with his adversaries in mildness and patience." [16]

In short, the priest must lead an exemplary life, a life that

[13] *Ibid.*, 6: 11 f.
[14] See II Tim. 2: 22–24.
[15] See I Tim. 4: 7 f.
[16] *Ibid.*, 6: 11.

will serve as a model and an incentive to others. His holy way of life and his steady advance in virtue should be clearly visible to the faithful. To this effect St. Paul again admonished Timothy: "Neglect not the grace that is in thee, which was given thee by prophecy, with imposition of the hands of the priesthood. Meditate upon these things, be wholly in these things: that thy profiting may be manifest to all. Take heed to thyself and to doctrine: be earnest in them. For in doing this thou shalt both save thyself, and them that hear thee." [17]

3. But still more in his official position and in his ministry must the priest, according to the admonitions of the Apostle, be a model of virtue and holiness to the faithful. After the example of our Lord, his duty consists in preaching the Gospel, in particular the Christian moral law, not only in words but also and primarily in deed and by his whole life. His entire life must be a mirror of virtue and perfection, in which the faithful can see the duties they owe to God, to their fellow-men, and to themselves. Every priest, standing before the flock entrusted to his guidance, should be able to apply to himself and his flock the words of the Apostle: "Be ye followers of me, as I also am of Christ." [18]

In another place, St. Paul again exhorted Timothy to the duty of giving good example: "Be thou an example of the faithful in word, in conversation, in charity, in faith, in chastity." [19] Writing in the same vein to Titus, he said: "In all things show thyself an example of good works, in doctrine, in integrity, in gravity, the sound word that cannot be blamed." [20]

[17] *Ibid.*, 4: 14–16.
[18] See I Cor. 4: 16.
[19] See I Tim. 4: 12.
[20] Tit. 2: 7 f.

In substance, these admonitions of St. Paul agree perfectly with the advice given by the supreme shepherd of the Apostolic Church, St. Peter, to the heads of the early Christian communities: "The ancients [i. e., priests] therefore that are among you, I beseech, who am myself also an ancient, and a witness of the sufferings of Christ: as also a partaker of that glory which is to be revealed in time to come: feed the flock of God which is among you, taking care of it, not by constraint, but willingly, according to God: not for filthy lucre's sake, but voluntarily: neither as lording it over the clergy, but being made a pattern of the flock from the heart." [21]

These words deserve to be taken to heart by all who have been admitted into the sanctuary and by all who are still striving toward that goal. The important point which both Apostles are unanimous in stressing is that the priest's way of life must fully coincide with his teaching. How easily a priest may destroy all he has built up by his preaching and teaching, if his personal life gives offense and scandal! The lukewarm portion of his flock is only too ready to regulate itself according to the lax conduct and life of its shepherd rather than according to his teaching and admonitions. On the other hand, a priest who is pure in intention and edifying in behavior exercises a salutary influence upon his people; in the fullest sense of the word he has become a pattern of his flock.

St. Paul lays special emphasis upon the conscientious administration of the office of preacher, seeing therein an excellent aid in the sanctification of the priest himself. With all possible earnestness he writes to Timothy of this duty:

[21] See I Pet. 5: 1–3.

"I charge thee, before God and Jesus Christ, who shall judge the living and the dead, by his coming, and his kingdom: preach the word: be instant in season and out of season: reprove, entreat, rebuke in all patience and doctrine. For there shall be a time, when they will not endure sound doctrine. . . . But be thou vigilant, labor in all things, do the work of an evangelist, fulfil thy ministry." [22] His advice to Titus is the same: "These things speak, and exhort and rebuke with all authority," [23]

In all his duties, but especially in his office as preacher of the word, the priest must strive to present himself "approved unto God, a workman that needeth not to be ashamed, rightly handling the truth." [24] The content of his preaching, however must not be the wisdom of the world or the cleverness of men, but solely the traditional doctrine in all its soundness and purity. This is the way in which St. Paul himself preached; he came not "in loftiness of speech or of wisdom"; his purpose was to impart to his hearers no other knowledge than that of Christ crucified. Therefore he despised all the artifices of rhetoric and contented himself with the "showing of the Spirit and power." [25]

And so, pointing to himself he directed the warning to Timothy: "Hold the form of sound words, which thou hast heard of me in faith, and in the love which is in Christ Jesus. Keep the good thing committed to thy trust by the Holy Ghost, who dwelleth in us." [26] In the same strain he wrote

[22] See II Tim. 4: 1–5.
[23] Tit. 2: 15.
[24] See II Tim. 2: 15.
[25] Cf. I Cor. 2: 1–5.
[26] See II Tim. 1: 13 f.

to Titus: "The sound word that cannot be blamed: that he, who is on the contrary part, may be afraid, having no evil to say of us." [27]

But no matter how zealously and successfully the apostolic laborer may work in word and example, he must never, as St. Paul warns, think of ascribing the success to himself; he must always be conscious that God is the one who blesses the work and lets it bear fruit; the worker himself is but an imperfect tool in the hands of God. The finest ornament of a laborer in the Lord's vineyard is therefore a spirit of profound humility and self-abasement: "What then is Apollo, and what is Paul? The ministers of him whom you have believed; and to every one as the Lord hath given. I have planted, Apollo watered, but God gave the increase. Therefore, neither he that planteth is any thing, nor he that watereth, but God that giveth the increase." [28]

4. If we glance back once more over the moral and vocational demands St. Paul makes upon the priest, we must admit that they presuppose a considerable amount of virtue and perfection. What he requires has not the character of a pious counsel which the individual is left more or less free to follow according to his own good pleasure, nor did St. Paul have an unattainable ideal in mind. He was thinking of a priestly personality *in concreto,* that is, as it should find its realization in priestly vocation. Every priest can and should, with the grace of God, reach the high moral level demanded by St. Paul.

That the Apostle was in earnest about his demands and

---

[27] Tit. 2: 7 f.
[28] See I Cor. 3: 5-7.

that he considered them not as pious counsels but as strict duties binding in conscience, is attested by the peremptory direction found toward the end of his first letter to Timothy: "I charge thee before God, who quickeneth all things, and before Christ Jesus, who gave testimony under Pontius Pilate, a good confession, that thou keep the commandment without spot, blameless, unto the coming of our Lord Jesus Christ." [29]

And so, the figure of the great Apostle confronts the priests of today, proclaiming with authority the law of personal sanctification and exhibiting in his own life the outstanding virtues that priestly holiness must embrace. Like perhaps no other, St. Paul, who stood on the threshold of Christianity and had been called by God Himself a "vessel of election," [30] grasped the profound meaning of the priesthood and the duty of personal sanctification that flows from it. The mind of St. Paul regarding the moral holiness demanded of every priest remains authoritative for all servants of the sanctuary.

4. TESTIMONY OF THE FATHERS AND OF THE CHURCH

1. As a second argument in proof of our thesis that personal holiness is absolutely necessary for the priest, we call upon some of the early fathers to give their testimony. St. Ephraim the Syrian says: "If thou, O brother, art honored with the priestly office, then endeavor by purity, righteousness, divine wisdom, and resplendent virginity to please Him who has chosen you. Be an ardent zealot like the virtuous

[29] See I Tim. 6: 13 f.
[30] Acts 9: 15.

Joseph; be as chaste as Josue, as hospitable as Abraham, a friend of the poor like Job, a tender lover like David, and in meekness like unto Moses." [81]

St. Gregory Nazianzen argues in this fashion: "A man must himself be cleansed before cleansing others: himself become wise, that he may make others wise; become light, and then give light: draw near to God, and so bring others near, be hallowed, and then hallow them; be possessed of hands to lead others by the hand, of wisdom to give advice." [82] In another place he says: "And before a man has, as far as possible, gained this superiority, and sufficiently purified his mind, and far surpassed his fellows in nearness to God, I do not think it safe for him to be entrusted with the rule over souls, or the office of mediator (for such, I take it, a priest is) between God and man." [83]

St. John Chrysostom writes as follows: "Wherefore his [i. e., the priest's] soul ought to gleam with beauty on every side, that it may be able to gladden and to enlighten the souls of those who behold it." [84] And again: "For the soul of the priest ought to be purer than the very sunbeams, in order that the Holy Spirit may not leave him desolate, in order that he may be able to say, 'Now I live, and yet no longer I, but Christ liveth in me' (Gal. 2:20)." [85] And still again: "And wherever he [the priest] invokes the Holy Spirit, and offers the most dread sacrifice, and constantly handles the common Lord of all, tell me what rank shall we give him? What great purity and what real piety must we de-

---

[81] De sacerd., cap. 8 (Assemani, Ephr. Syr. opera graece, III, 5).
[82] De fuga, cap. 71 (PG, XXXV, 480).
[83] Op. cit., cap. 91 (PG, XXXV, 493).
[84] De sacerd., I. 3, cap. 14 (PG, XLVIII, 650).
[85] Op. cit., I. 6, cap. 2.

mand of him? For consider what manner of hands they ought to be which minister in these things, and of what kind his tongue which utters such words? And ought not the soul which receives so great a spirit to be purer and holier than anything in the world?" [36]

In St. Gregory's *Pastoral Rule* we read: "The ruler [of souls] should always be pure in thought, inasmuch as no impurity ought to pollute him who has undertaken the office of wiping away the stains of pollution in the hearts of others also; for the hand that would cleanse from dirt must needs be clean, lest, being itself sordid with clinging mire, it soil whatever it touches all the more." [37]

In another passage of the same book we read: "The ruler [of souls] should always be chief in action, that by his living he may point out the way of life to those that are put under him, and that the flock, which follows the voice and manners of the shepherd, may learn how to walk better through example than through words. For he who is required by the necessity of his position to speak the highest things is compelled by the same necessity to exhibit the highest things. For that voice more readily penetrates the hearer's heart, which the speaker's life commends, since what he commands by speaking he helps the doing of by showing." [38]

2. The mind of the Church on this important question is fully in accord with the testimony of the fathers, and is expressed particularly in the conferring of major orders and in countless ecclesiastical decrees and instructions.

Through the mouth of the consecrating bishop the Church

[36] *Loc. cit.*, cap. 4.
[37] *Reg. Past.*, II, cap. 2 (PL, LXXVII, 27).
[38] *Loc. cit.*, cap. 3.

gives the following solemn warning to the candidates for subdiaconate: "If hitherto you have been remiss in coming to church, be henceforth diligent; if hitherto drowsy, be henceforth wakeful; . . . if hitherto lacking in purity, be henceforth chaste. . . . See whose ministry is given to you." [39]

While conferring diaconate, the Church utters this fervent prayer: "Let the practice of every virtue abound in them, mild authority, constant modesty, the purity of innocence; and the observance of spiritual discipline. In their conduct let thy precepts shine forth, so that the people may follow, in holy imitation, the example of their chastity." [40]

With still greater solemnity she addresses the candidates for the order of priesthood: "In truth, with great fear should one ascend to so high a rank, and care should be taken that heavenly wisdom, approved morals, and a long observance of righteousness should commend those chosen thereunto. . . . Let the perfume of your life be the delight of the Church of Christ; so that by your preaching and example you may build up the house, that is, the family of God. . . . Let your conduct be in conformity with the action you perform." [41]

In the countless major and minor synods that have been held in the course of the centuries, the sanctification of the clergy constituted a continually recurring chapter. The so-called *reformatio in capite,* so often discussed in the general councils, had to do primarily with the moral reformation and the virtuous life of the clergy, both high and low. As a matter of principle, the Church demands of her clergy a higher degree of morality and virtue than that expected of

[39] *Pontificale Romanum, de ordine subdiaconi.*
[40] *Ibid., de ordine diaconi.*
[41] *Ibid., de ordine presbyteri.*

the laity, incorporating in her canon law the dictum of St. Jerome: "It is gravely ruinous to the Church of Christ when the laity are better than the clergy." [42]

With the same idea in mind, the canon law in force today requires in a general way that priests lead, both inwardly and outwardly, a holier life than laymen, and that they hold before the latter the light of virtue and of good example.[43]

The Church desires only sinless and holy priests. Not many years ago Pope Pius X again gave expression to the ardent yearning of the Church in this respect. In his famous pastoral exhortation, addressed to the Catholic clergy of the whole world on the occasion of the fiftieth anniversary of his ordination to the priesthood, the venerable jubilarian in the Chair of St. Peter wrote these memorable words: "The difference between the priest and any righteous layman must be as great as that between heaven and earth; for that very reason priestly virtue must be guarded against stain, not only from the defilement of grievous sins but even from the slight blemishes of very small faults." [44] This particular letter of Pius X, which deals in detail with the personal sanctification of the priest, is alive with the spirit of the Church, the mystical bride of Christ, and merits the close and prayerful study of every priest.

We have purposely presented only a few authoritative witnesses to bear testimony to the fact that the priest is bound to labor unceasingly at his own personal sanctification. But the few we have adduced are ample to bring home to us the gravity and strictness of this obligation. If we were

[42] *In epist. ad Tit.*, cap. 2 (*PL*, XXXVI, 590); cf. *Corpus iur. can.*, can. 21, c.8, q.1.

[43] CIC, can. 124.

[44] *Acta S. Sed.*, XLI (1908), p. 560.

to cite all the admonitions of popes and bishops, of general and particular councils, of great saints and theologians, exhorting the clergy to personal holiness, and if we were to add the many admonitions to a holy priestly life, contained in the ascetic literature of recent years and of earlier times, we would never finish, even though we contented ourselves with the briefest summary. From every side the same warning-cry is heard: *Sancti estote!*

5. NATURE AND EXTENT OF PRIESTLY SANCTIFICATION

After what has been said, the fact that the priest, by his very vocation, has the duty of striving after virtue and holiness cannot be doubted. Moral holiness, however, has various degrees and can be understood in various ways. Hence the last question before us concerns the nature of the holiness and the degree of virtue and perfection to which the priest is obligated by his vocation. The word "holiness" has a threefold meaning: we speak of habitual, moral, and heroic holiness.

1. Habitual holiness is the first and lowest degree. By it we mean the simple possession of the state of grace, that is, freedom from mortal sin. In this sense, every person who possesses sanctifying grace can be called a saint. For the essence and effect of this grace is precisely to cleanse the soul from mortal sin and make it holy and pleasing in the sight of God. As a matter of fact, the early Christians were called by the Apostles with the significant name "saints." St. Paul, in particular, was fond of this appellation and used it repeatedly in his Epistles. To him the Christians were without more ado "called to be saints." [45]

[45] Cf. Rom. 1: 7.

The expression is sublime in content, and fully justified, though it has passed out of general use today. The new life which grace imparts consists essentially in the interior transformation and sanctification of the soul. Therefore St. Paul had reason to write to the new converts at Corinth: "But you are washed, but you are sanctified, but you are justified in the name of our Lord Jesus Christ, and the Spirit of our God." [46] He was thinking of baptism, which brought about this transformation as a result of the infusion of grace. And actually, every person on whose brow the waters of baptism have flowed and who later has never desecrated his soul by mortal sin may be called a saint. He possesses divine life, partakes of the nature of God Himself, is a reflection of the holiness of God, and has a right to the eternal company of the triune God in heaven. In short, such a soul stands in the right supernatural relation to God, in the relationship desired by God Himself; he is worthy of the special consideration and the fatherly love of God. He is a "new creature," [47] born again of water and the Holy Ghost.

We are aware that a thousand dangers from within and from without menace this holiness and that, as a consequence of the weakness and the guilt of man, it is often lost. The real significance of the sacrament of penance lies in this, that it gives back, by the mercy of God, to the fallen but contrite sinner the grace and holiness he had lost by sin.

Unquestionably the priest as the steward of Christ and the dispenser of the mysteries of God is strictly bound to possess this lowest and fundamental degree of holiness. It would be an inner contradiction and a profanation of divine things, if

[46] See I Cor. 6: 11.
[47] Gal. 6: 15.

he who at the altar celebrates the New Testament sacrifice *in persona Christi,* he who by virtue of his office as the servant of the Church and the representative of Christ administers the sacraments to give grace and supernatural life to others, were himself without this grace and without this supernatural life. What would be the awful consequence? Such a priest who celebrates mass, consecrates the sacred species, and receives holy communion in the state of mortal sin makes himself in an extraordinary manner "guilty of the body and of the blood of the Lord" and, as St. Paul puts it, "eateth and drinketh judgment to himself, not discerning the body of the Lord." [48] Precisely in the place from which all grace and salvation flow, he would call down upon his own head the curse of heaven, and open up to himself the fount of eternal damnation. This is a thought so terrible that it can hardly be fully grasped. Except in case of necessity, a priest in mortal sin cannot regain the state of grace necessary for the celebration of mass by making an act of perfect contrition which, in other instances, would restore the life of grace. To insure the holiness of the sacrifice and the worthiness of its celebration, the Church expressly prescribes that a priest, conscious of mortal sin, must, if possible, go to confession before he celebrates mass.[49]

In like manner, a priest who baptizes or hears confessions when not in the state of grace plunges himself from sin to sin. In these cases again, how terrible! While he looses the chains that fetter the souls of others, he clamps these same chains more tightly and securely about his own soul; while he pronounces the words of forgiveness and absolution over

[48] See I Cor. 11: 29.
[49] Cf. *Conc. Trid.,* Sess. XIII, cap. 7.

others, he utters over his own unhappy soul the sentence of eternal doom; while he opens to others the doors to eternal life, he opens more widely to himself the gates to eternal death.

When the seminarian pictures to himself these appalling possibilities, his soul no doubt is seized with fear and terror. But it is a salutary fear; it will induce him to test his vocation with all the more rigor and to refrain from entering the sacerdotal state carelessly and without the necessary moral qualification. He will come to understand how necessary it is for him, even in the years of preparation, to avoid sin, particularly mortal sin, to battle with all his energy against his evil inclinations and passions, and to take the conquest of self and the mortification of his sensuality seriously. This ascetic self-education in which the grace of God and personal effort must co-operate, may not be deferred until his later priestly life. Least of all may he imagine that salvation in this respect will come automatically with ordination and the sacramental grace of the priesthood; his soul's sanctification is his own personal task, and he cannot begin work at it too early. Long before ordination he must have acquired in conscience the moral certainty that, by using the appropriate natural and supernatural means, he can remain continuously in the state of grace, that he can live free of mortal sin. Otherwise the risk would be too great and the responsibility too unbearable.

2. The preservation of the state of grace is the more assured, the more closely the second grade of holiness, the moral, is joined to the first. By the second degree of holiness we mean the state of habitual virtue, that is, a disposition of soul that is acquired with the help of God's grace by the

sustained practice of virtue, a disposition that places a person in the position to perform good and virtuous actions with greater ease and consistency, just as if they had become second nature to him.

Such a disposition of soul, firmly establishing a person in virtue and making him inclined to the good, just as others by sin are inclined to evil, is not conferred automatically with the state of sanctifying grace itself; it is the result of sustained and purposeful co-operation between the free will of man and actual grace. The practice of virtue is difficult for a person in the beginning, even when he possesses and preserves sanctifying grace. For in spite of this grace and the holiness it effects in the soul, the perverse sensuality of man remains, the concupiscence which St. Paul calls the "law of the members." [50] This uncanny evil force that lurks in the dark depths of fallen human nature contradicts reason and grace. The Church teaches that concupiscence, while not sin, comes from sin and leads to sin.[51] It is the bleeding wound from which nature suffers as the result of original sin, a wound that is not healed by the grace of justification. According to the disposition of an all-wise Providence, the wound and the weakness are left in human nature, so that they may provide man with an opportunity for spiritual combat and supernatural merit.

And this is the point where the road of self-sanctification begins, a road leading up the steps of the moral virtues to the heights of personal holiness. The battle against one's own lower nature, humble denial of self, and persistent self-control, constitute in every case, also in the case of priestly

---

[50] Cf. Rom. 7: 23.
[51] Conc. Trid., Sess. V, n.5.

virtue, the first step on which everything else necessarily depends. And after this first step has been taken, the individual must never forget that all further striving after virtue must also be accompanied by the practice of these same fundamental virtues. Without humility and self-denial, sustained progress in virtue is simply impossible.

To treat adequately the wide range of priestly virtuous practices and to set forth in detail the specific priestly virtues that must be added to the general Christian virtues, is the province of ascetic theology. We wish merely to emphasize again the fact that the priest as priest is obligated to a more than average striving after virtue. In a very general way, the Church demands that even the simple cleric, who has been inducted into the clerical state by the reception of tonsure, lead a holier and more virtuous life than the layman, and that he serve as an example to the laity. How much more is this true of the consecrated priest whose hands have been anointed with the holy oil of ordination! Therefore the cleric, particularly the priest, cannot content himself with keeping free from mortal sin. Even the layman is obliged to do that, The cleric, *a fortiori* the priest, must go far beyond this minimum requirement; he must be zealous in cultivating a higher life of virtue. This higher obligation, of course, has not the same absolutely indispensable character as that which binds him to preserve the state of grace, that is, to avoid mortal sin. For without the state of grace he would not be able to exercise his office except unworthily and sacrilegiously, whereas the priest who, though not striving after greater virtue, at least keeps himself in the state of grace would perform his priestly functions both validly and worthily, that is, without mortal sin. But experience shows that such a minimum of moral worthiness cannot be preserved in the long run unless the priest cultivates a life of virtue, at least to a certain extent. Hence, from this vocational consideration alone, he is bound to a more than average practice of virtue and to the pursuit of holiness.

However, let us disregard this more conditional necessity for the moment. Would it not, as a matter of fact, be the sign of a base and unpriestly frame of mind, if the priest were to strive after moral holiness merely because he is driven to such effort by the necessity of preserving the state of grace, which barely keeps him free of the guilt of sacrilege, and if he were impelled by no positive or higher motive? Wherever a priest has a lively consciousness of the sublime dignity of his vocation, he will feel the necessity and the duty of a more than average life of virtue. The more a genuine priest, with the passing years, comes to a realization of what he is and what he should be, and the more he appreciates the meaning of his consecration and mission, so much the more will he be convinced of the necessity to strive uninterruptedly after holiness and so much the more will he be filled with a great desire for such holiness. When, however, the consciousness of vocation and mission has lost its effect and has been superseded by a spirit of indifference and smugness, striving after an increase in virtue also ceases. Then the individual consoles himself with the soothing but unwarranted reflection that striving after a higher degree of holiness is, after all, not the duty of the secular priest, but only of the religious.

In this place we merely observe that, according to ascetic theology, the religious as such belongs to the *status perfectionis acquirendae,* while the priest who participates in the office and duties of the bishop belongs, together with the bishop, to the *status perfectionis acquisitae et communicandae*. Accordingly, he is even more obligated to perfection by his very vocation, than is the religious.

3. In conclusion, we must add a word about the third degree of holiness, holiness in the sense of heroism. This is the holiness of the saints in the strict sense, whether they have been canonized or not. Holiness in this sense of the heroic practice of virtue is the concept of holiness most familiar to us; when we speak of saints, we mean holy persons of this type. The Church has never demanded of her children such a high degree of holiness as a strict duty, not even of her priests, even though she holds it up to priests and laity alike as the highest moral ideal, and teaches on principle that it is attainable with the help of God's grace. And in fact very many of her children have actually arrived at this perfect holiness.

Nevertheless, no matter how lofty and how desirable this ideal sanctity may be, we cannot assert that striving after it is an unconditional duty for anybody, or that without such effort a person would not be able to lead a good Christian life, or a priest would not be able to lead a good and virtuous priestly life. The Church always remains temperate in her fundamental and unconditional demands. Even with regard to the priesthood she does not go beyond the limits of what every priest by dint of earnest desire and effort can attain in the way of virtue and perfection. The Church in her commandments is content to set the boundaries of the necessary and the obligatory; beyond these limits she allows free play to the upward-striving free will of man and the sway of God's grace. We must always hold fast to the truth that a boundary line must be drawn where the domain of the obligatory ceases and the domain of evangelical counsels and works of supererogation begins, a dividing line separating command from counsel. Happy the priest who has been called by God to be a saint!

Index

Aaron, Priesthood of, 4
Abuses in the Church, 110 f.
Adam (Karl) on the mystical body, 54
Aloysius Gonzaga, St., 151
Altar: The priest at the, 32 f.; source of danger to priest, 188 f.
"Ambassador of Christ," The priest as, 85-88
Animae candidae, 156
"Another Christ," The priest, 20 ff.
Apocalypse on the lay priesthood, 15
Apostles: Calling of the, 9; Mission of the, 10 f.; Sending of the, 86; and the work of preaching, 26
Apostolate, Social character of the, 115
Arianism, 98
Arius, 183
Ars, Curé of: example for pastors, 174; zeal in the confessional, 192
Asceticism: Incentives to priestly, 87; Need of, 150
Augustine, St.: on the administration of the sacraments, 48; Church's debt to, 98
Austria, Episcopal foundations in, 101

Baptism, The priest and, 30, 56
Benedictines, and missionary activity, 118

Benefices, Purpose of, 107 f.
Bernard of Clairvaux, St., 94
Bible. *See* Scripture
Bishop, minister of holy orders and confirmation, 29
Bishops: and the duty of preaching, 26; and seminary training, 103
Boniface, St., Missionary activity of, 99, 118
Blessed Sacrament. *See* Eucharist
Blessed Virgin. *See* Mary
Breviary: Holiness of the, 204; Priest's obligation to recite the, 170
Brothers in the mission field, 99

Caiphas at the trial of Jesus, 12
Calling of the Apostles, 9
Cana, Christ at, 75
Candidates: *animae candidae,* 156; drawn to pastoral ministry, 130; need of idealism, 152; need of self-examination, 190; need of unselfishness, 152; Two groups of, 156; Unfit, 152; *see also* Seminarians
Canonical impediments, Purpose of, 104
Canon Law, New Code of: on clerical privileges, 106 f.; on the duty of pastors toward candidates, 101; on seminary training, 102
Care of souls. *See* Ministry, The pastoral

231

Catechism of the Council of Trent. *See* Roman Catechism

Celibacy in the Latin Church, 151

Character, Indelible, 40, 72

Charity: and the faults of the Church, 111; and the pastoral ministry, 173

Chastity: Dangers to, 196 f.; Questions of conscience and, 198

Christ

At Cana, 75

Command to preach, 26

And the difficulties of the pastoral ministry, 128

Divinity of, 5, 39

Doctrine of the mystical body, 54 f.

Eternal priesthood of, 45

Founder of the Christian priesthood, 1-13

Friendship for Lazarus, 75

The good shepherd, 34

Our high priest, 5, 22

And holiness, 200

Idea of vocation, 86

Light of the world, 67

Man of God, 74

As mediator, 88 f.

Minister of His heavenly Father, 82

Mission of, 7, 23

On the nature of His kingdom, 134

On the necessity of suffering, 129

On the need of battle, 81

On the need of self-denial, 148

And the people, 116

Personality of, 22

And poverty, 148

Priesthood of, 20-25

Priest's analogy with, 39 ff.

Priest's relationship to, 20 ff.

Purpose of mission of, 116

On self-denial, 141

Christ (*continued*)

And the sons of Zebedee, 153

Threefold mode of existence, 50

Unique character of, 5

On the value of the soul, 126

Virginity of, 149

And the world, 147

Christianity: opposed to the world, 134; the religion of joy, 175; and true freedom, 154

Christ's kingdom, Supernatural nature of, 23, 135

Church

Concern about clerical training, 100-104

Dangers confronting the, 79

Debt of, to the priesthood, 97

Holy Eucharist and the, 33, 51

Interest of, in profane fields, 97

Mission of the, 8

And morality, 28

Prayers of, for her priests, 104

Priesthood and the, 92-114

Priest's attitude toward, 109-14

And the training of seminarians, 73

Church history, Clerical scandals in, 184

Chrysostom, St. John: on the burden of the priesthood, 164; on the dignity of the priesthood, 60 f.; on the mass, 47; on priestly holiness, 218; reluctance to receive holy orders, 198

Civil forum, Priests and the, 106

Civitas Dei, 135

Civitas terrestris, 135

Clergy, Privileges of the, 107 f.

Clerical garb: honorary privilege, 107; a protection to the priest, 174

Clericus, Meaning of the word, 137

Clerus, Meaning of the word, 137

Cologne, Synod of (1860), on dignity of the priesthood, 53

Compromise, Dangers of false, 137

Concupiscence, Practice of virtue and, 226

Confessional, The priest in the, 191 ff.

Confirmation, administered by the bishop, 29

Congregations, Missionary, and the monastic ideal, 119

Conscience, Chastity and questions of, 198

Consecration of the priest's person, 205-209

Consolations in the pastoral ministry, 37, 171 f.

Council of Trent. *See* Trent, Council of

Councils, Seminary training and Church, 103

Co-worker of God, The priest as a, 36

Criticism, Evil spirit of, 110

Cross: Christ as our mediator on the, 90; The mass and the, 46; Sacrifice of the, 24

Curé of Ars: in the confessional, 192; example for pastors, 174

Cure of Souls. *See* Ministry, The pastoral

Dangers inherent in priesthood, 180-99

Deacons in the early Church, 26

Death: of the good priest, 178; of the wicked priest, 183

Defense of the Church, committed to priesthood, 98

Deus scientiarum of Pius XI, 103

Dignity of the priesthood, 43-63

Dionysius (pseudo-Areopagite), on the pastoral ministry, 124 and note

Direction of souls, 38

Divine power: of Christ, 40; of the priest, 41

Divinity of Christ, 5, 39

Domestic life of the priest, 146

Dress, Clerical, 107, 174

Dupanloup (bishop), on the difficulties of the pastoral ministry, 128

Duties, The priest's essential, 25 ff.

Dying, The priest and the, 32, 56

Economics in relation to the pastoral ministry, 123

Education in relation to the pastoral ministry, 123

Eloquence, Dangers of pulpit, 196

Ember days, Significance of, 104

Ephraim, St.: on the dignity of the priesthood, 59; on priestly holiness, 217

Essence of the priesthood, 7, 20-42

Essential duties of the priest, 25 ff.

Eucharist: The Church and the, 33, 51; entrusted to the priesthood, 12; The priest and the, 31, 49 ff.

Example, The priest and good, 213

Exodus on the lay priesthood, 13

Extreme unction, The priest and, 32, 56

Faultfinding, Dangers of, 110

Forbidden books, The seminarian and, 145

France, Catholic universities in, 102

Francis of Assisi, St., 135, 151

Francis Xavier, St., 99

Freedom, Christianity and true, 154

Garb, Clerical: privilege of the priest, 107; protection to the priest, 174

Germany, Episcopal foundations in, 101

Golgotha, Christ on, 24

Good example: The priest and, 213; St. Paul on need of, 76; St. Peter on need of, 214

Good shepherd, Christ as the, 34

"Good soldier of Jesus Christ," The priest as, 78-81

Grace: and the free will of man, 170; the life of the mystical body, 55; The priest as mediator of, 29; The soul and sanctifying, 126

Gregory the Great, St. (pope): on the character of the priest, 77; on priestly holiness, 219

Guidance of souls, 38

Heaven, The good priest's hope of, 177

Hermits, Secular priests contrasted with, 118

Hettinger: on the mass, 32 f.; on priestly consolation, 168; on renunciation of the world, 137

Hierarchy, Institution of the, 9

High priest: Christ our, 5, 22; Liturgical vesture of Jewish, 71

History, Clerical scandals in Church, 184

Holiness
  Of the breviary, 204
  Christ's demand for, 200
  Duty of the priest, 48, 200-30
  Habitual, 222-25
  Heroic, 229
  Of the mass, 202 f.
  Mind of the Church on priestly, 219 f.
  Moral, 225
  Nature of priestly, 222
  Pius X on priestly, 221

Holiness (continued)
  Of the priest, 200-30
  Of priestly functions, 201 ff.
  Of the priestly state, 200-205
  Of the priest's teaching, 204
  St. Ephraim on priestly, 217
  St. Gregory the Great on, 219
  St. Gregory Nazianzen on priestly, 218
  St. Jerome on priestly, 221
  St. John Chrysostom on priestly, 218
  St. Paul's admonitions to, 209 ff.

Holy Eucharist. See Eucharist

Holy orders: administered by the bishop, 29; character indelibilis, 40, 72; Effect of, 165; power to consecrate, 49; Sacramental grace of, 167 f.; Symbolism of, 206 f.

Holy Spirit, Conferring of the, 165

Holy Writ. See Scripture

Honorary titles, Priest's right to, 107

Human side of the Church, 111

Humility: necessary in the priest, 172, 195; St. Paul on priestly, 216

Immortality of the soul, 125

Impediments, Purpose of canonical, 104

Incarnation, Purpose of the, 23

Innocent III (pope), Civil supremacy of, 135

Internal conflicts in the life of a seminarian, 140

Inviolability, Clerical, 106

Jeremias (prophet), Tribute by Onias to, 90

Jerome, St.: and asceticism, 151; on priestly holiness, 221

Jesus. See Christ

Joy: Christianity and true, 175; in self-control, 159

Judgment, The priest and the, 178, 183

Kingdom, Supernatural nature of Christ's, 23

Lay co-operation, Need of, 96

Lay priesthood: Apocalypse on the, 15; Exodus on the, 13; in the liturgy of the mass, 15 f.; and the priesthood of orders, 9, 13 ff., 21; Protestant view of, 16 f.; in the Psalms, 16; St. Paul on the, 15; St. Peter on the, 13, 15

Lazarus, Christ's friendship for, 75, 149

Liberalism: condemned by Pius IX, 69; and the seminarian, 145

"Light of the world," The priest as, 67

Lippert: on the Catholic priesthood, 5 f.; on the indelible character of the priesthood, 166; on the mission of the priest, 87; on secular leaders, 166

Liturgy: Holy Eucharist in the, 51; Lay priesthood in the, 15 f.

Love of souls, necessary in priest, 35

Loyalty to the Church, 114

Luther, 183

Lutheranism, 98

"Man of God," The priest as, 40, 70-75

Mankind, Needs of, 121

Marriage and the sex instinct, 197

Mary: and the incarnation, 39; Words of consecration and the fiat of, 50

Matrimony, Administration of, 29

Mass: Fruits of the, 168 f.; Hettinger on the, 32 f.; Holiness of the, 202 f.; Lay priesthood in the liturgy of the, 15 f.; The priest and the, 32 f., 46; renewal of Christ's death, 46; St. John Chrysostom on the, 47

Mediator: Christ as, 88 f.; The priest as, 88-91

Mediatorial office: of the Jewish priesthood, 89; Protestant view of, 89

Meditation, necessary for the priest, 170, 190

Military service, Exemption of clerics from, 106

Mind of the Church: The priest and the, 109 f.; on priestly holiness, 219 f.

Ministry, The pastoral, 34 ff.
   Aids to, 122
   Benedictines and, 118
   Christ on the difficulties of, 128
   Consolations in, 37, 171 f.
   Curé of Ars and, 174
   Difficulties in, 37, 127, 171 f.
   Dionysius (pseudo-Areopagite) on, 124 and note
   Dupanloup (bishop) on difficulties of, 128
   Field of, 119
   Man's soul the object of, 122
   Monastic orders and, 118
   Motive in vocation, 130
   Needs of present day, 96
   Province of, 121
   Ramifications of, 123
   Rewards in, 129, 173
   St. Gregory Nazianzen on, 124
   St. Paul on, 127

Ministry (*continued*)
School of charity, 173
Source of blessing to priest, 171
Sublimity of, 35 ff.
Mission: of Christ, 7, 23; of the Church, 8; of the priesthood, 8
Missioner, The priest as, 99
Missions, Foreign: Brothers and nuns in, 99; Priesthood's contribution to, 99
Monastic ideal, Missionary congregations and the, 119
Monastic orders and missionary activity, 118
Monks, Secular priests contrasted with, 118
Moral law, The priest and the, 27
Morality, The Church the guardian of, 28
Mortal sin, The priest and, 224
Mystical body: Adam (Karl) on the, 54; Grace the life of the, 55; and the priesthood, 8; Priest's power over the, 53-57; St. Paul on the, 8, 53 f.; in the teaching of Christ, 54 f.

Naturalism, condemned by Pius IX, 69
Nature of the priesthood, 20-42
Nazianzen, St. Gregory: on the pastoral ministry, 124; on priestly holiness, 218; reluctance to receive holy orders, 198
Nuns in the mission field, 99

Obedience, Duty of, 113
Omne bonum a clero, 93
Omne malum a clero, 93
Onias (high priest), tribute to Jeremias, 90
Original sin, Results of, 139 f.

Pagan influences at work in world, 69
Pastoral ministry. *See* Ministry, The pastoral
Pastoral needs of the present day, 96
Pastoral Rule of St. Gregory the Great, 77, 219
Pastors: duty toward candidates, 101; duty of preaching, 27; example of the Curé of Ars, 174
Patrick, St., 99
"Pattern of the flock," The priest as, 75 f.
Paul, St.
On the administration of the sacraments, 28 f., 48
Admonitions of, 209 ff.
On the dangers of secularism, 124
On the duty of preaching, 26, 215
Example of priestly holiness, 217
On the folly of the world, 133
On good example, 76
On the holiness of the priesthood, 210
Identity with Christ, 167
On the incarnation, 40
On internal conflict, 156
On joy in tribulation, 176
On the law of the members, 140
On the lay priesthood, 15
List of priestly virtues, 212
Missionary zeal, 117
On mortification, 151
On the mystical body, 8, 53 f.
And pastoral activity, 117
On the pastoral ministry, 127
On the priesthood and the Church, 95
On priestly humility, 216
On spiritual armor, 80
Vocation of, 26

Peace, the portion of good priests, 168

Penance, The priest and the sacrament of, 30 f., 56

Persecution, Christ on, 176

Personality of Christ, 22

Peter, St.: on good example, 214; on the lay priesthood, 13, 15; on the reward of good priests, 129; on sanctifying grace, 126

Philosophy, The priesthood's contributions to, 98

Pius IX (pope), condemnation of liberalism and naturalism, 69

Pius X (pope), on priestly holiness, 221

Pius XI (pope), *Deus scientiarum*, 103

Politics in relation to the pastoral ministry, 123

Popes: Civil supremacy of the, 135; Influence of the, 68 f., 96; and the training of seminarians, 102

Potestas jurisdictionis, Roman Catechism on, 44 and note

Potestas ordinis, 44

Poverty: of Christ, 148; The priest and, 108; and the secular priest, 150

Prayer in the life of the priest, 171, 190

Preaching: Bishops and the duty of, 26; Christ on the duty of, 26; Dangers in, 196; Pastors and the duty of, 27; Sacred character of, 204; St. Paul on the duty of, 26, 215

Precedence, Clergy's right to, 107

Priest

And the administration of the sacraments, 28 ff., 97

At the altar, 32 f., 188 f.

As the ambassador of Christ, 85-88

Priest (*continued*)

Analogy with Christ, 39 ff.

"Another Christ," 20 ff.

Attitude toward women, 197

And baptism, 30

And the breviary, 107, 204

Celibacy and the, 151

Champion of the moral law, 27

And chastity, 196 f.

And the civil forum, 106

Coadjutor of God, 127

In the confessional, 191-94

Consecration of the person of the, 205 ff.

Conviction of a divine sending, 165

Co-worker of God, 36

Danger of a worldly spirit in the, 73, 211

Death of the good, 178 f.

As director of souls, 38

And domestic arrangements, 146

Duty to meditate, 170

Duty of personal holiness, 48, 66, 72

Duty of preaching, 26

Duty of renouncing world, 137

And the dying, 32, 56

Essential tasks of the, 25 ff.

And extreme unction, 32

And good example, 213

As a good soldier of Jesus Christ, 78-81

And habitual virtue, 225 f.

Harm done by wicked, 98

Heavenly reward of the good, 177

And the Holy Eucharist, 49 ff.

Identity with Christ, 167

And the judgment, 178

As the light of the world, 67

Lippert on the mission of the, 87

Love for the Church, 112

Love for the world, 133

Priest *(continued)*
  Love of poverty, 147
  Love of souls, 35
  Man of God, 40, 70-75
  Man of prayer, 171
  Mediator of God and men, 88-91
  Mediator of grace, 29
  Minister of Christ, 82
  As missioner, 99
  And mortal sin, 224
  And the mystical body, 53-57
  Need of fidelity in the, 84
  Need of humility in the, 172
  Need of tact in the, 112
  Need of unselfishness in the, 172
  Participation in priesthood of Christ, 45
  Pastoral Rule on the character of the, 77
  As the pattern of the flock, 75
  And poverty, 108
  Prayer of the Church for, 104
  And preaching, 195 f.
  The priesthood and the, 160-99
  Recreation of the, 146
  Relationship to Christ, 20 ff.
  Reward in store for good, 76
  And riches, 108, 147
  And the sacrament of penance, 30 f.
  As the salt of the earth, 65 f.
  And secular pursuits, 162
  And self-denial, 141 f.
  Servant of Christ, 83
  Shepherd of souls, 34 ff.
  And sin, 191, 194
  And the state of grace, 223 f.
  As teacher, 25 ff.
  Unworldliness of the, 142 f.
  World's hatred for the, 133
  And zeal for souls, 37
Priesthood
  Of Aaron, 4

Priesthood *(continued)*
  Blessings of the, 164-80
  Of Christ, 20-25, 45
  And the Church: duty of love, 112; duty of obedience, 113; duty of loyalty, 113 f.; duty of tact, 112; St. Paul on, 95; Schrörs on, 93 f.; thinking with the Church, 109 f.
  Church's debt to the, 97
  Dangers inherent in: association with holy things, 188 f.; to chastity, 196 f.; Confessional as a source of, 191; Irrevocability of the priestly state, 185 ff.; Service of the altar, 188 f.; Success in preaching, 196
  Defender of morality, 28
  Defender of the Church, 98
  Dignity of the: Church fathers on, 57 ff.; Roman Catechism on, 62 f.; St. Ephraem on, 59; St. John Chrysostom on, 60 f.; Synod of Cologne (1860) on, 53
  Divided allegiance, impossible in the, 161
  Divine origin of, 1 ff.
  Essence of, 7, 20-42
  External. *See* Priesthood of orders
  General. *See* Lay priesthood
  The heart of the Church, 93
  And the Holy Eucharist, 12
  Human side of, 2
  Instituted by Christ, 1 ff.
  Irrevocable nature of, 185 f.
  Jewish: Christian priesthood foreshadowed by, 4; duty of holiness, 209; End of the, 13; Exclusiveness of, 4, 116; Holiness of, 206; Mediatorial activity of, 89; Priesthood of Christ and the, 12; Sacred character of, 71

Priesthood (*continued*)
Of the laity. *See* Lay priesthood
Lippert on the Catholic, 5 f.
Mission of the, 8
And the mystical body, 8
Nature of the, 20-42
Objective holiness of the, 200-205
Of orders: Lay priesthood and
the, 9, 21; Catholic teaching
on, 17 f.
Pagan, 3
And the people, 115-31
And the priest, 160-99
A protection to the priest, 174
St. Paul on the holiness of the,
209 ff.
Secular: contrasted with monas-
ticism, 118; danger of secu-
larism, 123 f.; and the pas-
toral ministry, 119; Personal
sanctification and the, 119;
Poverty and the, 150
And secular pursuits, 161
And secular vocations, 1 f.
Social character of the, 115-20
Unchanging nature of the, 2
Unique character of, 161
Visible. *See* Priesthood of orders
And the World, 115, 132-59
Priestly functions, Holiness of,
201 ff.
Priestly spirit, Lack of, 188
Priests, Unworthy, 182
Private baptism, in case of neces-
sity, 29
Privileges, Clerical: *privilegium
canonis,* 106; *privilegium
competentiae,* 107; *privilegium
fori,* 106; *privilegium im-
munitatis,* 106
Prohibition of books, Purpose of,
145
Protestants: false view of medi-
atorship, 89; and the lay priest-
hood, 16 f.

Psalms on the lay priesthood, 16

Questions of conscience, Chastity
and, 198

Rademacher on Christ's attitude
toward world, 147
Real body of Christ, Priest's power
over, 49 ff.
Recreation, The priest and legiti-
mate, 146
Renunciation of the world: Mean-
ing of priest's, 138 ff.; Necessity
of, 141-47; Hettinger on, 137
Revealed truth, The priest and, 25
Reward in store for the priest, 129:
St. Paul on, 180; St. Peter on,
76
Rewards in the pastoral ministry, 173
Riches, The priest and, 108, 147
Rite of ordination, 105
Roman Catechism: on the dignity
of the priesthood, 62 f.; on the
potestas jurisdictionis, 44 and
note; on the priesthood, 6
Roman colleges, 102

Sacerdos alter Christus, 20 ff.
Sacramental grace of holy orders,
167 f.
Sacraments, Administration of: baptism, 56; confirmation, 29; extreme unction, 32; Holiness
demanded by, 203; Holy Eucharist, 31, 56; holy orders, 29;
matrimony, 29; meritorious for
the priest, 170; penance, 30 f.,
56; The priest and the, 28 f.,
47; reserved to priests, 97; St.
Augustine on, 48; St. Paul on,
28 f.
Sacred Scripture. *See* Scripture
Sacrifice, Idea of, 3
Sacrifice of the cross, Infinite value
of, 25

Saints, Heroic virtue of, 229

"Salt of the earth," The priest as, 65 f.

Salvation, The priesthood no guaranty of, 181

Sanctification of the priest, 200-30; St. Paul's demands, 209 ff.

Sanctifying grace: Holiness and, 222; Priest must retain, 223 f.; St. Peter on, 126; The soul and, 126

Sanhedrin, Trial of Christ before, 12

Saul, Vocation of, 26

Scandals in history of the Church, 110 f., 184

Schrörs on the priesthood and the Church, 93 f.

Scripture: on the calling of the Apostles, 9; on the correct attitude toward the world, 132; on the mission of the Apostles, 10; on the priesthood, 64-91; on the rewards for good priests, 130

Secchi (Angelo), priestly astronomer, 162

Secular priesthood, Social character of, 115 f.

Secular problems, Church's concern in, 97

Secular pursuits, The priest and, 161 f.

Secular vocations: Adaptability of, 160; Changing character of, 1

Secularism, Danger of, to secular priests, 123 f.

Secularization: of Church property, 144; of the clergy, 144, 211

Seipel (Ignaz), priestly statesman, 163

Self-denial: Fruits of, 153 f.; Need of, 141 f.; a source of joy, 159; Thomas à Kempis on, 158

Seminarians
    Attitude toward world, 144, 155

Seminarians (*continued*)
    And the avoidance of mortal sin, 225

Choice of vocation, 120

Dangers of faultfinding, 110

Drawn to pastoral ministry, 130

Duty of loyalty, 113

Duty of obedience, 113

Duty of renouncing world, 137

Duty of self-denial, 156

And forbidden books, 145

Internal conflicts and, 140

Love for the Church, 112

Need of asceticism, 88

Need of confidence, 159

Need of heroism, 79

Need of struggle, 156

Need of tact, 112

Training of: avoidance of mortal sin, 225; Bishops and the, 103; Canon law on the, 102; Church councils and the, 103; Church's concern in the, 73, 100-104; Council of Trent on the, 101; Discipline of the mind and heart, 158; Forbidden books, 145; Pius XI on, 103; Popes and the, 102; Thinking with the Church, 110

And the worldly spirit, 144 f.

Wrong conception of vocation, 120

See also Candidates

Seminaries: Council of Trent on establishment of, 101; Early origin of, 101

Seminary, Apostolic college the first, 10

Sex instinct, Control of the, 197

Shepherd of souls, The priest as, 34 ff., 120-31

Sin and the priest, 191, 194

Social character of the priesthood, 115-20

Soul: Christ on value of the, 126;

Soul (*continued*)
  Immortality of, 125; Sanctifying grace and the, 126
State of grace, The priest and the, 223 f.
Steward, The priest as, 84
Suffering, Necessity of, 129, 176
Supernatural character of the priest, 39 ff.

Tact, essential in priest, 74, 112
Tertullian, 98
Theology: Pius XI on study of, 103; Priesthood's contributions to, 98
Thomas à Kempis on self-denial, 158
Thomas Aquinas, St., Church's debt to, 98
Trent, Council of: on the establishment of seminaries, 101; on the priesthood of orders, 11

Unfit candidates, 152
Unselfishness, necessary in the priest, 172
Unworthy priests, 182

Vanity, reprehensible in the priest, 195

Vincent de Paul, St., 94
Virginity of Christ, 149
Virtue, The priest and habitual, 225 f.
Virtues, St. Paul's lists of priestly, 212
Vocation: Choice of, 120; Christ's idea of, 86; Zeal for souls a sign of, 37

Women, The priest's attitude toward, 197
World: Christ's conquest of, 136; Correct attitude toward, 132; Hatred for, 132 f.; Love for, 132 f.; Moral retreat from, 136; Pagan spirit of, 69; The priesthood and, 115, 132-59; Renunciation of the, 134
Worldly pleasures, The priest and, 146
Worldly priests, Menace of, 144
Worldly spirit: reprehensible in the priest, 73; Seminarians and the, 144 f.

Zeal for souls: necessary in the priest, 37; St. Paul and, 117; a sign of vocation, 37
Zebedee, Sons of, Jesus and the, 153

ORDER FORM

Quantity Discount

1 copy   3.75

5 copies   3.25 each

10 copies   3.00 each

25 copies   2.75 each

50 copies   2.50 each

100 copies   2.25 each

Gentlemen:

Kindly send me _____ copies of **The Priesthood** by Most Rev. Wilhelm Stockums. Enclosed is my payment in the amount of _____.

Name_____

Street_____

City_____

State_____ Zip Code_____

Order from . . .

TAN BOOKS AND PUBLISHERS, INC.
P.O. Box 424
Rockford, Illinois 61105